ROCKHOUNDING
Colorado

ROCKHOUNDING
Colorado

Fourth Edition

WILLIAM A. KAPPELE

REVISED BY GARY WARREN

FALCONGUIDES

ESSEX, CONNECTICUT

FALCONGUIDES®

An imprint of Globe Pequot, the trade division of
The Rowman & Littlefield Publishing Group, Inc.
4501 Forbes Blvd., Ste. 200
Lanham, MD 20706
www.rowman.com

Falcon and FalconGuides are registered trademarks, and Make Adventure Your Story
is a trademark of The Rowman & Littlefield Publishing Group, Inc.

Distributed by NATIONAL BOOK NETWORK

Previous editions of this book were published by FalconGuides in 2017, 2004, and
1998.

Photos by Gary Warren unless otherwise noted.
Maps by Melissa Baker and The Rowman & Littlefield Publishing Group, Inc.

British Library Cataloguing in Publication Information Available

Library of Congress Cataloging-in-Publication Data Available

ISBN 9781493067909 (pbk. : alk. paper) | ISBN 9781493067916 (epub)

∞™ The paper used in this publication meets the minimum requirements of
American National Standard for Information Sciences—Permanence of Paper for
Printed Library Materials, ANSI/NISO Z39.48-1992.

In Memory: Keltsie Lynn Mansfield (1995–2015). As we were approached to revise this book we were excited about the prospect of visiting and photographing the rockhounding sites in Colorado. We planned on leaving for Colorado in June of 2015 to start the revision of the book. On April 15, 2015, we tragically lost our granddaughter in a horrific act of domestic violence. To suffer such a loss was a devastation to our family but after a while we found it necessary to begin the work on this book. Though it was difficult to begin, we found it to be an enjoyable endeavor and because Keltsie enjoyed going rockhounding with us, we decided to dedicate this book to her and donate part of the money from the book sales to a fund to support domestic violence awareness. It is our hope that through this maybe another family can be spared the heartbreak we have experienced.

—Gary and Sally Warren, 2016

CONTENTS

Southwestern Colorado

Southeastern Colorado

Overview

ACKNOWLEDGMENTS

It is impossible to thank all those who helped make this book a reality. So to all the fine people to whom we talked in stores, motels, town halls, gas stations, ranger stations, Bureau of Land Management (BLM) offices, and even a hospital, we offer our deepest thanks.

I must thank W.R.C. Shedenhelm, editor emeritus of *Rock & Gem* magazine, who first made it possible for me to write about having fun and even getting the writing published. Thank you W.R.C., I am grateful that after all these years, I can still have fun writing about having fun.

Without the help of Darlene and Joe Reidhead of Durango, Colorado, a lot of the pages in this book would be blank. They introduced Cora and me to four-wheeling many years ago, and the virus has taken up permanent residence in our systems.

Thanks, too, to Connie Bishop of Bloomfield, New Mexico, who told us of trips in Colorado, including the one to the picture stone in La Plata Canyon, which we had walked past without seeing on numerous occasions.

A very special thanks goes to Gary Curtiss, a geologist with the Colorado Department of Natural Resources and a major resource for this book. Gary performed above and beyond the call of duty in putting real "ite" names to the "pretty stuff" we had picked up.

Also in line for special thanks are Mary Amelotte, geology technician; Peter Borella, professor of geology and oceanography; and Jim Repka, assistant professor of geology, all of whom are from Saddleback College in Mission Viejo, California. These good folks also helped with mineral identification—particularly the beautiful piece in the cover photo.

Finally, thanks to my wife and coauthor, Cora, without whom not only this book, but nearly everything I have ever done would not have been possible. She visited every site in the book, and her eagle eye turned up a lot of the material described. Cora can sit down on a log and find more rocks, minerals, and artifacts within a three-foot radius than I can by hiking for miles. When I return with an empty bag and sore feet, she just smiles and shows me her treasures. As if this were not enough, when we get back to the task of writing, she assumes the thankless task of proofreading every word. I guess I'd better buy her a quarter pounder with cheese and a vanilla shake.

—William A. Kappele

I also need to thank all of the people that helped with the revision of this great book.

Some of my great friends helped by going with my wife Sally and me and helped explore and verify the sites in this book. Larry and Marsha Christophersen who helped verify sites in the southeastern part of the state, and Dave and Kathy Farnsworth who helped us verify sites in the northeastern and southwestern parts of Colorado.

We had many good times with them and it helped us get through the long days and many miles we traveled in preparing to rewrite this book. I would also like to thank the people at our new site in this book, at Last Chance Mine (Site 50). The owner, Jack Morris and his staff were very helpful in not only giving us information about this site but also in helping us understand the area around Creede and the many mines within this area. In Del Norte, Colorado, on Twin Mountains (Site 51), we have to say that we were confused as to where to go and stopped at the home of Mark Boyd and he put aside his work and took us to the sites listed in Twin Mountains. He also showed us where there were ruins of an old French—yes, French—fortification in this area and also a wall where the French hid from the Indigenous people until all but two were killed off and they left the area. This happened many years before the Spanish came into the area; so, there is really a history in this area worth exploring.

There were many other people who took the time to talk with us and help us find sites, and though we cannot name them individually, we are grateful to these people also. The people of Colorado were very courteous to us and were always willing to talk and help us. My thanks go out to all of them for their help and kindness. And finally I want to say a big thank-you to my wife who put up with me on these trips and has helped me revise this book. Without her help this would not have been possible to accomplish.

—Gary Warren

Map Legend

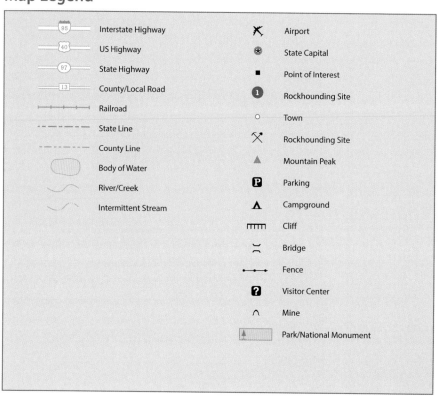

Interstate Highway	Airport
US Highway	State Capital
State Highway	Point of Interest
County/Local Road	Rockhounding Site
Railroad	Town
State Line	Rockhounding Site
County Line	Mountain Peak
Body of Water	Parking
River/Creek	Campground
Intermittent Stream	Cliff
	Bridge
	Fence
	Visitor Center
	Mine
	Park/National Monument

ABOUT THIS BOOK

Anyone who has followed the rockhounding hobby for more than a few years has undoubtedly encountered the two most common types of guidebooks. First is the one that simply lists the material to be found, gives brief directions to the sites, and provides a map that may or may not be accurate. The second type is more a treasure house of adjectives than a guidebook. Although the material to be found at the site may look as interesting as a piece of broken sidewalk, it will invariably be described as containing "fiery" reds, "deep, rich" purples, "breathtaking" oranges, and so on and on. Many rockhounds (including the two of us) have driven down miles of dirt roads and hiked over hills and through valleys only to be disappointed because the enthusiasm of the guidebook's author outdid the actual beauty of the find. We will not so mislead you in this book. If we are describing a site where red agate can be found, we will call it red agate even if we might think it is "fiery." You will have to be the judge, since beauty certainly is in the eye of the beholder.

Some guidebooks list old sites that are no longer productive. Some sites, in fact, have been rockhounded into oblivion and would not yield enough material for a 30 × 40 cabochon with the use of heavy equipment. This is not to say that old sites are not worth visiting, however. Many still provide worthwhile cutting material or mineral samples, but it is not just a matter of leaning out the car window and picking them up. We have listed some of these sites, but we also tell you just how hard and long you may expect to work for your prizes.

For this fourth edition of *Rockhounding Colorado,* we have dropped the number of sites from eighty-three to eighty-one. The sites have been modified to take into consideration the closing of private land and the opening or closing of mines. In the section on "Fifteen Trips for the Intrepid Explorer," GPS coordinates have been added to each trip.

All of the sites in this book have been carefully checked for accessibility. We will not send you to a site that is part of a national monument, nor have we listed any sites that are now underneath a shopping mall. We have also been extremely careful to indicate when a site is on private land. While much of central and western Colorado is public land, the eastern part is mostly private. Farmers and ranchers are generally willing to let you collect on their property if it will not disrupt their activities, but you must always ask. Just because there is no posting does not mean that collecting is allowed. It is also important to understand that all sites, and particularly mine sites, are subject both to fluctuations in mineral prices and the whims of their owners. One day a mine may look as though no one has been near it in a hundred years, but within a short time it could be reopened and working.

It is hard to keep up with this roller coaster when you live in the area, but if you live a hundred or a thousand miles away, it is virtually impossible. The status of public lands can change, too. Spots that have been open to collecting for years can become parts of various "protected areas." Forest roads can be closed to protect property rights of folks who own private property within the forest boundaries, fires and floods can close roads or whole areas, and public lands can be sold or leased.

We know from experience that for the rockhound, there is no feeling quite as bad as the one you get after driving a long distance with the expectation of some nice collecting only to see the dreaded "Keep Out" sign. The best way to avoid this feeling is to check out the site status before starting. To make this task easier, we have included contact information at the back of the book for Bureau of Land Management (BLM) field offices, national forest ranger districts, and government offices for all sixty-four Colorado counties. A phone call to one of these could save you a lot of disappointment.

We have included several of the famous mining districts for old mine buffs, but because of the always changing collecting status, we have purposely not listed any specific mines in these districts, with a few exceptions. We have listed some specific mine sites where we are pretty certain that collecting will be allowed—but it's still a good idea to check before going.

Both the authors and the publisher feel there is a lot more to the hobby of rockhounding than simply collecting rocks and hauling them home to fill up the backyard or the garage. The facets of the hobby are many and varied. There are collectors who only want to pick up pretty rocks and take them home for displays or for the rock garden. Often these people do not even know the kind of material they are collecting. Many do not care. That's fine. Some rockhounds are locked into the agates and jaspers and would walk over a mountain of mineral specimens and not even see them in order to get to their favorites. Some collect only what they can use their lapidary skills on, and others want mineral specimens for display or micromounting. There are even those whose interest is in the geology of the area and who don't care if the native rock does look like pieces of broken sidewalk. In short, rockhounds come in many flavors, and we have tried to offer something of interest to all.

Happy hunting! We hope that you have as much fun using this book as we did in researching and writing it.

INTRODUCTION

Called the Centennial State because of its admission to the Union 100 years after the US Declaration of Independence of 1776, Colorado is a rectangular plot of ground 387 miles from east to west and 276 miles from north to south. At 104,247 square miles, it is the eighth largest of the fifty states. Colorado shares borders with Wyoming, Nebraska, Kansas, New Mexico, Utah, Oklahoma, and about an inch and a half of Arizona down in the Four Corners area. Enclosed within these borders is a land of contrasts.

The state's geology ranges from the high plateaus of the west through the magnificent 14,000-foot peaks in the central section to the vastness of the Great Plains in the east. While not the largest state, Colorado takes first place as the highest. The lowest point in the state is 3,350 feet at the intersection of the Arkansas River and the Kansas state line, while the highest is Mount Elbert at 14,433 feet. Mount Elbert, though, is only one of fifty-three peaks in the state over 14,000 feet. In addition almost 900 peaks are at least 11,000 feet. All of these skyscrapers help give the state an average altitude of nearly 7,000 feet.

In Colorado, 60 percent of the land is privately owned, which is not necessarily good for the rockhound, but the remaining 40 percent is held by federal, state, and local governments, which is generally good for rockhounds. Federal lands include the Arapaho, Roosevelt, Gunnison, Grand Mesa, Uncompahgre, Routt, Pike, San Isabel, Rio Grande, San Juan, and White River National Forests. Collecting, with some minor restrictions, is allowed in all of these forests. In addition to the national forests, the BLM administers 13,000 square miles of public lands. As it is in the national forests, collecting, with a few restrictions, is allowed on BLM land.

The federal government also administers four national parks in the state: Mesa Verde, Rocky Mountain, Black Canyon of the Gunnison, and Great Sand Dunes National Parks. No collecting is allowed in the national parks, nor is it allowed in the national monuments or national wilderness areas. Colorado has six of these: Colorado, Florissant Fossil Beds, Hovenweep, Canyon of the Ancients, the Colorado portion of Dinosaur National Monument, and Browns Park (added to this list in February 2015).

To do justice to the formation of the mountains, plains, and plateaus that we call Colorado would take a book in itself. This is not a geology text, however, so we will include only the briefest overview of how the sites (and sights) you will be visiting came to be.

During the Mesozoic Era, about 200 million years ago, what are now the Eastern Plains were covered with warm, shallow waterways filled with marine life. As the water levels rose and fell, layers of shale were deposited. Eventually, erosion of the Rockies deposited great quantities of debris on the plains, covering the shales that contained the remains of marine plants and animals. Finally, the movement of the North American Plate sliding over the Pacific Plate caused the land in much of the southwest to rise an average of about 5,000 feet. It is in this area, where the ancient shale layers are exposed today, that we search for fossils of those long-departed marine animals and plants.

While all of this was taking place on the plains, dinosaurs were roaming in a lush, tropical climate graced with warm rivers and lakes and dense forests in what would one day become central and western Colorado. Unfortunately for the dinosaurs, but fortunately for us, many of the dinosaurs were trapped in layers of mud, silt, and volcanic ash where, over eons, the cell structure of their bones was replaced by silica. Thus they were preserved for those of us who would come along millions of years later to collect and study the fossilized remains of those huge beasts.

At the end of the Cretaceous Period, about 65 million years ago, when the dinosaurs were almost extinct, the North American and Pacific Plates came together, causing stresses in the central region. The resulting upheaval created the mountains that today we call the Rockies. Over the centuries that followed, more stresses caused fractures in the Earth's crust, which allowed magma to flow upward. Some of this magma formed the San Juan Mountains in Colorado's southwestern corner, while other flows filled cracks and crevices and caused them to fracture. These fractures were filled with a wide variety of minerals in solution. Most of this process, called hydrothermal mineralization, occurred along a wide area from a spot in Boulder County southwest to San Juan, Hinsdale, La Plata, and Mineral Counties. The area is known as the Colorado Mineral Belt and contains most of the famous old precious-metals mining areas.

Has all of the violent upheaval that formed the Earth as we know it stopped? Will we become the fossils of a million years hence? Will our agatized hip sockets become the earrings for a rockhound of the future? Better get out and find a fossil before you become one.

A WORD ABOUT THE WEATHER

You will notice that often we list spring through fall as the best seasons for collecting. This is very general, however, since the weather varies greatly from one region to the next, from one altitude to another, and from year to year. Generally because of the high altitude of Colorado, you can start getting into the mountains in late May or June and need to get out by October. On one day in late June 2015, we went from 100 degrees Fahrenheit in Grand Junction to 35 degrees Fahrenheit in Silverton.

On the Eastern Plains, summers can be hot and severe thunderstorms, often with hail, are common. Tornadoes are also frequent visitors to the plains. We decided on one trip that you know you may be in trouble when the telephone book in the motel has instructions on what to do after a tornado. Don't let this keep you from going, though. If you worry about every natural disaster that might befall you, you will spend your life hiding under the bed.

The Western Plateau has temperatures closer to those of the high desert areas of eastern Utah. Summer days often top 100 degrees Fahrenheit in many places. If you are used to desert collecting, this may not bother you; but if you don't like the heat, you will be much happier collecting in the spring or fall.

The mountainous spine through the center of Colorado presents a very different situation. At some of the higher sites, it is not uncommon to have snow showers in July. Weather in the high country can change in the blink of an eye, and lightning is a real concern at or near the peaks. You may well start out with a beautiful cloudless sky, and by the time you arrive at your destination, be in either a downpour or a snowstorm. One year we were camped in La Plata Canyon. For three days in a row, the one-hour hike to an old mine began under a beautiful blue sky and ended in pouring rain.

Even though there are weather situations to be aware of, most of the time it is beautiful in Colorado. We visited more than a hundred sites in a little over two months in researching this book. We went out every day and were rained out only one time. So gather up your rock bags and hammers and head out. Colorado is a place you will never forget.

FINDING YOUR WAY

We have made every effort in this guidebook to provide accurate maps with usable landmarks and all highway and road designations. The mileages given in the text are as accurate as the odometer on our vehicle. The major problem is that even on freeways, odometer readings will vary, and on jeep roads where the wheels are constantly bouncing, readings are notoriously bad. Thus the mileage figures must be taken as approximate. Whenever possible we have included prominent and reasonably permanent landmarks.

Because of the difficulty of building roads to most of the mines, these routes change very little. In some areas, however, there may be a new fork here and there that didn't exist when the map was drawn. Usually these new roads are readily identifiable as new, but once in a while a little backtracking is necessary. It is not only part of the fun, but you just might make a new discovery.

We have included descriptions of the types of roads to all of the sites. On some, the family sedan is fine; but much of the time a pickup or other high-clearance vehicle is needed; and for some, four-wheel drive is absolutely necessary. Check the type of road and make sure you have the right vehicle before you start. We will not lead you into trouble. If we err, it will be on the side of more vehicle than you need rather than less.

Part of our assignment in revising this book was to include GPS coordinates, take color photos, and verify that there is still material at the sites to be found. All GPS reading are done with WPS 87, which is the readings you get when you take your GPS out of the box. This is the setting that is common to all GPS instruments. As you take the reading for these sites, make sure that you are not under any trees and that you have a number of satellites showing on your GPS. The more you have the more accurate your readings will be. In doing the GPS readings, we did not go to everywhere there was material, rather we did the GPS reading at parking areas where you will start your search.

One of the other problems that we found in revising this book was the number of miles that you would have to travel from one site to another, so we have changed the site numbers to maybe simplify finding the different sites listed in this book. We have divided Colorado into four sections with the Continental Divide being the centerline from north to south and then using I-70 as the dividing line from east to west. This will put sites into a northeast, northwest, southeast, southwest grid.

SAFETY TIPS

ABANDONED MINES

The dangers that exist around abandoned mines would appear to be apparent, but many people just seem to forget. They forget, for example, that falling down some of the old deep shafts would be similar to falling off a tall building. Because the distance is not readily visible, the danger is masked. All shafts, portals, and drifts should be avoided. Many of the old mines have been left to the elements for nearly a hundred years, and the shoring has probably rotted away. The engineering in many of the mines was often hit or miss to begin with, so many of the mines may not have been safe even when they were originally opened. Colorado has been aggressively pursuing a plan to put steel gates or gratings over the most accessible shafts and portals, so the danger is significantly lessened, but there are still some that are open and inviting. The best advice is to never enter an abandoned mine. Decayed timbers and open shafts are only two of the many hazards.

Most of the mountain mines are wet, and pools can sometimes be deceptively deep. It is not unheard of for someone to drown in a mine. Bad air is another possibility, bringing the danger of suffocation. One thought should keep any sane person out of such danger: If there were riches worth risking life or limb for down in the depths, then why was the place abandoned?

Children must be watched constantly. Naturally, they have to be kept away from the underground workings, but there are many more kinds of trouble they can get into. Many of the sites listed in this book, and virtually all of the mines, are on steep mountainsides. In addition, the tailings piles are steep and often unstable. A slide down a large pile could result in broken bones and other serious injuries. Some of the sites in this book are by very busy highways with not much room to roam, so make sure that you watch for vehicles while rockhounding in these areas.

All of this gloom is not meant to keep you from exploring these fascinating spots for fear of disaster. There is no reason why such exploration cannot be safe and pleasurable. A good dose of caution and common sense can ensure that it will be.

MOUNTAIN DRIVING

We assume that all rockhounds are aware of the simple safety rules for our hobby, so no attempt will be made to lecture on such things as donning safety goggles and wearing hats in the summer sun. However, a few driving precautions in the mountains can mean the difference between an enjoyable trip and disaster. If you are new to driving in the mountains, take a minute to absorb the following information.

Many of the old mine and jeep roads are one lane with only occasional pullouts for passing. If you drive roads like this for long, you will, sooner or later, meet another vehicle going the opposite way. And there will be no pullout. This is one of those situations that we all dread, but they will happen, and it is important to know just how to handle them when they do.

Remember the most important rule: The vehicle traveling uphill has the right of way. The reason for this is that it is much more dangerous to back down a hill than up one. It is easy for a vehicle backing down to get out of control.

Try to remember where the turnouts are. It will help your peace of mind if you have to back up to one. Keep an eye out for approaching vehicles as far ahead as you can. Even though you may be going uphill, if you see a vehicle coming and you can pull over near where you are, you may prevent a confrontation. Unfortunately, not all drivers are this courteous, and some will just keep coming as though the road will suddenly widen out. Finally, don't panic and don't try to pass by the other vehicle or let it pass by you, unless you are 100 percent certain that it is safe to do so. We have seen vehicles try to pass by driving onto the uphill bank and tipping dangerously. We have also seen them go perilously close to the drop-off. Just stay calm and, if you are in the vehicle headed downhill, back up slowly and carefully. Remember, the rocks will wait.

It is certainly not a crime to be a novice when it comes to backroad mountain driving, but it may well be a crime not to admit it. There will be times when you crest a hill and see only sky in front of you. The road drops down, but you cannot see it over the hood. The novice who thinks he is a pro will drive on, betting that the road is really there and that it doesn't take a sharp turn. The sensible driver will stop and have a passenger get out and take a look, or he will stop the engine, block a wheel with a convenient rock, and take a look himself. Doing this may seem "sissy" or too time consuming, but it can prevent an accident or even death.

A similar situation concerns shelf roads and others that would be difficult to back out of. There is a shelf road like this up behind the Aspen Mine (Site 39). It looks alright as it begins, but it rounds a blind curve and ends at a washout. It is barely one lane, and the drop-off is hundreds of feet. Having to back out of a situation like this is something no one wants to repeat. If you find yourself confronting a road where you are not sure of being able to turn around, get out and walk a ways. It will save you time, embarrassment, and possible serious injury. The bottom line in this kind of driving is this: If you aren't sure of the road condition, find out. If you can't find out, don't go.

WEATHER

Weather can change rapidly in the high country and you must be ready for it. If you are heading into the 11,000–12,000-foot levels, be ready for rain, hail, or snow, even in July and August. Be sure you have both rain gear and warm clothing. Have sunscreen, too. The sunlight isn't filtered as much at 12,000 feet as it is at sea level, and even though the sun may not feel hot, it will fry your bald spot or blister your nose before you are aware of it.

The weather can be a real problem for driving anywhere, but on a remote jeep road it can be much worse. Note the kind of surface on the road as you go. A road surface that looks like friendly dirt can become so slick in the rain that you might rather have ice. Old mine roads are given minimal maintenance at best, and rain that doesn't look too bad can cause washouts that will make it impassable. If you are in a remote area and rain is impending, think about the road you drove up on. Maybe you should pack up and leave. There is always another day to hunt for minerals, and it might be a long walk out if the road should wash out.

Don't let all of these gloomy prospects deter you from the fun of rockhounding in the high country, but do practice good old horse sense. It will make your experience one to look back on with pleasure.

TOOLS OF THE TRADE

As you go out on these excursions, there is one thing that everyone should have in their possession: tools to extract your treasures with. As I have been out rock hunting for many years, I have put together a bag of tools that I always pack wherever I go. The first and most important tool is a good rock hammer. These come in a variety of sizes and weights, so don't just settle for the first one that you see. Look around and choose a good one that fits your needs. Make sure that the weight of the hammer is right for you and it has a comfortable handle, as you are going to be using this a lot in just about every place you go in Utah.

The next item is a chisel. These also come in a variety of sizes. I have two that I take with me. One has a pointed tip and one has a flat tip, so depending on the situation, I have something to loosen the rocks. I have a pack of small screwdrivers that I use to check out cracks and fissures that may have small hidden gems in them. One with a nice long shank is especially helpful. These are also used for picking out smaller pieces of rocks. Make sure that you have a bag to place your findings in and something that you can wrap around your treasures to keep them from breaking. Take paper towels, tissues, or small baggies to help keep your treasures safe. If you are going after small gems, a pill bottle or two helps keep your gems from being lost or broken in your bag.

These items can be thrown into a backpack or small bag and should only weigh around 10 pounds. This way you can pack more. If you are going to be doing some hard digging, you will need to have a good shovel and pick and also a breaker bar to help get your rocks out of the ground. Remember, when you dig a hole be sure and cover it back up when you leave. These are just a few basic tools that I have, and where I am headed will determine what I pack, but these I usually have with me all the time. As you get out and start rockhounding in earnest, you will find tools that will suit your needs and can add them to your pack, but remember that you do not want to overfill your pack so that you cannot carry your finds with you. One of the places where I get my tools is a small company called Geo-tools; the owner has been into rock hunting for many years and knows what tools work best. Look it up on Geo-tools.com. I have a Wizard Wreaking bar and the Eastwing Paleo Pick from them, and they are great basic tools for the rock hunter.

You should always carry plenty of water, snacks, sunscreen, and a small first aid kit. Make sure someone knows where you are going because safety is the number-one concern.

One of the best tools that you can have with you is a GPS. This item can take you to your hunting spot quicker than you can try to figure out which trail or road to take. When I was asked to revise the first edition of this book, one of the revisions that they wanted was GPS sites. I had never really used a GPS instrument before, and I had a lot to learn. I took some classes, which are available, and picked areas to try and find with my GPS. I found that the GPS does rely on satellites, and if you do not get enough satellite signals with your GPS, you can be off a number of miles. One degree of latitude equals approximately 364,000 feet (69 miles), one minute equals 6,068 feet (1.15 miles), and one second equals 101 feet. One degree of longitude equals 288,200 feet (54.6 miles), one minute equals 4,800 feet (0.91 mile), and one second equals 80 feet. When you stop to take a GPS reading, as you start your GPS, a chart will come up on the screen telling you how many satellites your GPS is tracking. Make sure that you are receiving at least five so that your GPS reading will be fairly accurate. More readings are better. Another problem that you have in the mountains are trees, bushes, and mountains, of course. They can block out a signal and give you a bad reading. In looking at the website for *Rockhounding Colorado*, there were comments about the GPS readings being incorrect. In this edition, I have gone back and checked GPS readings and corrected any that were wrong, so I hope that this will help you find your treasure sites.

ROCKHOUND ETIQUETTE

It is an often overlooked fact that all land belongs to somebody. Those of us cursed with living in a city have no trouble with this concept when we are in our own areas. We don't question the fact that even the rare vacant lot is not available for public use. But when we get out into the wide open spaces, we sometimes forget that just because there is nothing on the land, and there are no "Keep Out" signs, permission to enter is not given automatically. Every square inch of the United States belongs to somebody.

In Colorado, about 60 percent of the land is privately owned. The rest is owned by federal, state, or local governments, with a small amount for Indian reservations. Each private owner makes his own rules for rock collecting, and each governmental agency does the same. If we are to be responsible rockhounds and keep the lands available to us, we need to know and follow the rules and regulations.

UNWRITTEN RULES

It is sometimes hard to remember, especially when hounding around some of the old mining areas, that we should try as much as humanly possible to leave the land looking as though we had not been there. If you do a lot of digging, fill in the holes before you leave. Don't dismantle old buildings, even if you do want to make picture frames or a coffee table with that beautiful weathered wood. Always leave gates as you find them. If the gate was closed, close it behind you. If it was open, even though it may seem wrong, leave it open. It should go without saying that you take out any trash you brought in, and it won't hurt if you take any that someone else may have left. The cleaner we keep these sites, the better the chances they will stay open.

BUREAU OF LAND MANAGEMENT

The BLM defines a rockhound as one who collects rocks, minerals, and fossils as a hobby. Collecting is permitted on all BLM lands with a few restrictions. First, the rockhound must not create a significant disturbance. This is a little vague, but common sense tells us that we should not dig to the point where we cause erosion of the land or pollution of streams or other water sources. Nor should we drive our vehicles on soft soil where the wheel tracks will create gullies and promote erosion. BLM regulations may have changed regarding some of the sites. Check current regulations for the sites that you plan to visit.

Small amounts of rock and mineral specimens are allowed to be collected, but "small" is not really defined. The rules are to differentiate between recreational collectors and commercial miners, so it seems that if you can lift your rock bag and carry it to your vehicle, you are probably okay. There are more specific rules for petrified wood. The limit is 25 pounds per day per person, not to exceed 250 pounds per year. Fossil collecting, too, has some special regulations. Except in designated areas, plant and invertebrate fossils may be collected without restriction. Vertebrate fossils, fish, and mammals may not be collected on BLM lands.

If you would like the latest information on the collecting status of various areas, or could use some directions or maps, drop in to the local BLM office. Check the local phone book or call or write to the BLM main office in Denver. The address and number are in Appendix C at the end of this book.

THE FOREST SERVICE

The Forest Service rules and regulations are essentially the same as those of the BLM. It does not have the 25-pound or 250-pound limit on petrified wood, but specifies small quantities. The fossil regulations for the Forest Service have changed. On April 17, 2015, the Forest Service enacted a law where you can no longer actively collect fossils of any kind on Forest Service land. If you are just walking down a trail and see a fossil lying there, you can pick it up, but you cannot use a hammer or chisel to get it out of a rock. There are those who are trying to repeal this regulation, but you will need to check the regulations before you go fossil hunting. Some of the sites have been deleted because of this new regulation.

STATE LANDS

Collecting is permitted in state wildlife refuges as long as there is no significant disturbance of the land and the collecting is for hobby purposes.

Roadcuts provide some very good collecting and are open, providing the digging does not cause the walls to slide onto the roadway, traffic is not disrupted, and safety is maintained.

PRIVATE PROPERTY

We cannot emphasize enough the importance of getting permission before collecting on private property. Owners of farms and ranches are usually very good about allowing those who ask to collect on their property, if it will not interfere with their operations. As we were revising this book, we traveled to many places where there are now large beautiful homes built near or on collecting sites in the old book. Remember that the first edition of this book was written in 1995 and many things have changed, especially private land and owners. At one of the sites we visited (by Boulder, Colorado), we went to where there were supposed to be mine tailing and found them in a fenced pasture with a large camel keeping watch over them. The real problem is with some of the land in the eastern part of the state. This prairie land is vast, and there are often no houses or anyone to ask for many miles. In fact, we found that in many cases the owners do not even live in the state. The only way to gain access to such spots is to go to the county recorder's office and try to find a name and address for the owner. This is a time-consuming process, but if the site looks particularly good, it might be worth the effort. Please resist the urge to enter the land just because no one is watching.

In the case of mines on public lands, it is reasonable to assume that if there is no posting and no signs of recent work, it is probably okay to collect. There is a small group of "miners" who feel that putting a sign of any kind on a rock site guarantees them access to half of the western United States. If you think this is the case, check it out at the local Forest Service or BLM office.

WHERE COLLECTING IS PROHIBITED

Collecting is not allowed in national parks, national monuments, or federal wilderness areas. Permission is granted only rarely for collecting on Indian reservations. The best rule of thumb for determining collecting status is to ask the owner, whether that is a private landowner or a government agency.

SIGHTS ALONG THE WAY

Most rockhounds are more than one-track minds with a hammer and bag. As a matter of fact, most are possessed with a great curiosity about a wide range of things. For this reason, we have included the following short list of side trips near the rockhounding sites.

AMES POWER STATION

If you are in the Four Corners area, and particularly in the vicinity of Alta (see "Fifteen Trips for the Intrepid Explorer"), you can visit the site of one of the most important events in the history of the modern world. In a little valley just off CO-145 stands the Ames Power Station. Passed by nearly all of the traffic on the highway, and largely forgotten in the history books, this little station was the producer of the first commercial alternating current in the world. This was the place that proved Nikola Tesla's theory, which makes possible the toasters, microwave ovens, electric razors, and, yes, even the computer that has produced these words and the printer that committed them to paper.

All of this was the idea of Lucien Nunn, a lawyer who had been hired to represent the owners of the Gold King Mine at Alta. The mine had been losing money and creditors were about to take it over. Nunn realized that the greatest financial problem was the cost of producing electric power. All electric power at that time was direct current, which was expensive to produce and could not be transmitted over long distances. He had heard of George Westinghouse's work on Tesla's theory and enlisted his help in building the power plant at Ames. Current was generated by the power of water flowing through a flume from Trout Lake, high above, running across a Pelton wheel that turned the generator. The inexpensive electrical current saved the Gold King. In fact, it was so successful that lines were strung clear across 13,000-foot Imogene Pass to power the mines around the Camp Bird Mine on the Ouray side of the mountains.

Finding the site: From the junction of the spur to Telluride and CO 145, drive south on CO 145 for about 10 miles. A road heads east to Ophir Pass, and a dirt road drops down into the valley to the west. Take the road to the west to the bottom of the hill and the power plant.

BLACK CANYON OF THE GUNNISON NATIONAL PARK

If you are in the areas of Whitewater (Site 25) or the Señorita Mine (Site 29), you can take a short drive to one of Colorado's most unusual geologic features. The Black Canyon of the Gunnison River is a 53-mile crease in the basement rock of the area. Composed primarily of schist, coarse granite, and gray quartz, the width of the canyon ranges from about 1,300 feet at the rim to a minimum of just 40 feet at the river. The depth varies from 1,730 feet to more than 2,000 feet. One area, called the Painted Wall, is 2,300 feet high, the highest such cliff in Colorado. The wall gets its name from intrusions of gray and pink bands of granite that filled cracks in its surface.

Of the 53 miles of canyon, 12 miles were set aside for a monument by President Hoover in 1933. On October 21, 1999, the monument became Black Canyon of the Gunnison National Park. Today, the monument includes 21 square miles of canyon and rim.

Finding the site: To reach the south rim of the canyon, drive east from Montrose on US 50 for 8 miles, then take CO 347 northeast for 6 miles.

CAVE OF THE WINDS

If you can tear yourself away from the fluorite of St. Peter's Dome (Site 79) long enough, you might want to visit the Cave of the Winds, a fine example of a limestone cave.

It is not clear just who first discovered the cave, but in 1879 and 1880 George Snider spent time exploring it. Soon after, he bought the land and opened the cave to tours. There are just under a mile of passageways, with many fine examples of limestone formations.

Finding the site: Leave I-25 at US 24 (exit 141) in Colorado Springs. Drive west on US 24 for 5.5 miles to the well-marked Cave of the Winds Road.

DINOSAUR NATIONAL MONUMENT

While you are in the Elk Springs area, you really should take the time to visit Dinosaur National Monument. The monument covers nearly 330 square miles and is a wonderland for both paleontologists and geologists. Although it is named for the dinosaurs, only a small part of the monument contains dinosaur fossils. The part that does, however, is truly amazing.

The part of the monument that draws most people's attention is the building containing the quarry wall. This wall contains scattered bones of these huge animals just as they were deposited on an ancient sandbar.

These are the bones of dinosaurs that died near a river and whose carcasses were carried down the river and trapped on the sandbar. Here they were probably set upon by scavengers, and their bones strewn about randomly. The river once again took over and carried the bones downstream where they were trapped on more sandbars.

Some of the bones were completely covered by the sand and, as the soft parts decayed and were replaced by silica, became fossilized. Over time tons and tons of sand, volcanic ash, and mud compressed the bone-containing layer and formed it into rock. At the time the fossilized layer was about a mile deep. After millions of years, both upheaval and erosion exposed the ancient sandbar with its treasure of fossils.

By a stroke of luck, just at the time when the fossil layer was well exposed, a scientist by the name of Earl Douglass happened by, in search of dinosaur fossils. He had been commissioned by Andrew Carnegie to find specimens for his new museum in Pittsburgh. It was well known that Morrison formations in both Wyoming and Colorado contained dinosaur fossils, but only a few reptilian fossils had been discovered in the Uinta Basin. On August 17, 1909, Douglass discovered eight tailbones of the brontosaurus and the hunt was on. Over the next 15 years, 350 tons of fossilized bone were removed and shipped to museums. In 1915, Douglass requested that the government enclose the remaining fossil layer in a building both to protect them and to give the public a place in which to view them. With customary speed and efficiency, the government went to work, and in 1958 the building was built.

In this building you can see a wall of more than 2,000 exposed fossil bones, which have been buried for 150 million years. If you are in the area, don't miss this sight, but make sure you leave the rock hammer behind; there is no collecting here.

Finding the site: Although most of Dinosaur National Monument is in Colorado, the visitor center and quarry are just across the state line in Utah. To reach the Dinosaur Quarry Visitor Center, go west on US 40 from the Utah/Colorado state line for about 20 miles to Jensen, Utah. At Jensen, take UT 149 north for 7 miles to the visitor center.

GARDEN OF THE GODS

This is another site near Colorado Springs. When you finish looking over the Cave of the Winds, you might want to see the Garden of the Gods, another geologic wonder just a few miles away.

As the modern-day Rocky Mountains were forming, great chunks of the plains were tilted up and formed hogbacks along what is now the Front Range. All of these formations are fascinating, but the Garden of the Gods outdoes them all. Eroded formations of conglomerate, gypsum, and sandstone resemble sculptures. Colors of red, white, and pink predominate. Perhaps the most visited of the formations is Balanced Rock. Although not the largest such formation in the world, it may be the most famous.

In 1909, the family of Charles Perkins donated the property to the city of Colorado Springs with the stipulation that it be open to the public and free of charge for all time. The Garden of the Gods is currently a city park.

Finding the site: To enter the park from the north, take exit 145 (Garden of the Gods Road) off I-25 east for about 2.5 miles to where the road dead-ends into 30th Street. Go left on 30th Street where it forks with Mesa Road. Then stay to the right on 30th Street for just less than a mile, where a well-marked road to the right leads to the park.

To enter the park at Balanced Rock, go west from I-25 on US 24 toward Manitou Springs. At 4 miles turn right onto Manitou Avenue and follow the signs to the park.

GEORGETOWN

Not far from the Genessee Dike (Site 15) you can view the reconstruction of one of mountain railroading's marvels, the Georgetown Loop.

In the late 1800s, Leadville was a booming mining area, but no railroad had yet been built to it. The wagon road from Georgetown was a long day's journey, so Jay Gould decided to run his Colorado Central & Pacific Railroad through Silver Plume and on to Leadville. The problem was that although Silver Plume was only 1.5 miles or so from Georgetown, it was about 600 feet higher. Consequently, the track ran up the valley on a shelf, made a hairpin turn back toward Georgetown, then made another hairpin turn over a 90-foot-high trestle (which came to be called the Devil's Gate Viaduct), and headed back to Silver Plume. It took 4.5 miles of track to go the 1.5 miles, but the grade did not exceed 3 percent, and it worked. Unfortunately, there were problems with the trestle, and it had to be taken down and rebuilt. By the time the trestle was finally ready, the Denver & Rio Grande had reached Leadville from Cañon City, so the Colorado Central & Pacific railway was never completed. The short line to Leadville did remain in use until just before World War II when the trestle was taken down and its materials were used for shoring the mines.

The famed Devil's Gate has been rebuilt, and an excursion train takes passengers on the thrill ride of their lives. Maybe you would like to give it a try.

Finding the site: Georgetown is just a few miles west of the Genessee Dike turnoff on I-70. At exit 228, a large sign directs you to the Georgetown Loop National Historic District.

IMOGENE PASS

If you go to the Señorita Mine in Ouray (Site 27), you might want to take a trip over Imogene Pass. At 13,114 feet, Imogene Pass stands between Ouray on the east and Telluride on the west, and is one of the highest passes in Colorado. It looks down on the Camp Bird Mine on the Ouray side and the Tomboy Mine on the Telluride side.

In the early 1900s, labor strife broke out in some of the mines around Telluride. Union members eventually forced nonunion miners to walk out and over Imogene Pass. The mine owners persuaded the governor to send in the National Guard to protect the nonunion workers and restore peace to the mines. In order to prevent the union members from sending in reinforcements, Fort Peabody was built at the top of the pass, and troops manned it through the winter of 1903–1904. Today a monument marks the spot. Even with modern machinery, snow keeps the pass closed for all but a few weeks each year. We can only imagine what a whole isolated winter up there must have been like.

The views from Imogene Pass are among the most spectacular in all of Colorado, but getting up there to see them is not a walk in the park. If you are not an experienced mountain driver, you may be better off taking one of the guided jeep tours that depart from Ouray. There are jeeps for rent in both Ouray and Telluride, but remember this is not a trip for a novice.

Finding the site: It is best to make local inquiries about the routes and about current road conditions. If the pass is closed, you could spend a lot of time driving to a dead end. There are also many old mine roads going in all directions. Most will rejoin the main road, but again, you could spend a lot of time chasing your tail. The jeep rental agencies can give you the best directions and road conditions.

MESA VERDE NATIONAL PARK

This is an easy side trip if you are exploring La Plata Canyon (Site 35) or the Cortez area (see "Fifteen Trips for the Intrepid Explorer"). This park should not be missed by anyone who is near the Four Corners area.

There is much to see on the 15-mile-long, 8-mile-wide Mesa Verde, but without question, the most spectacular sights are the great dwellings in the cliffs. These probably represent the pinnacle of the Anasazi ("Ancient Ones") culture. The Anasazi began on the mesa as hunters and gatherers. They used an arrow-throwing device called an atlatl to kill game and eventually cultivated corn and squash. Over many centuries, they began to settle in the caves on the cliff faces. This may have been to provide shelter from the weather or to make attack from enemies more difficult. Or it may well have been a combination of the two.

Whatever the reason, the beautiful ruins are there for all of us to see today, thanks largely to the tireless efforts of a group of women who formed the Colorado Cliff Dwellings Association and lobbied Congress for 25 years to establish a national park to protect this treasure. During the late 1800s and early 1900s, commercial ventures exploited the ruins and many antiquities were sold to collectors and tourists. Finally, however, Congress acted, and in 1906 the park was established.

Today serious archaeological exploration is still carried on by university researchers and other scholars. Most of the cliff dwellings are open to public tours, and such a tour is an experience not to be missed.

Finding the site: From Cortez drive east on US 160 for 10.5 miles to the well-marked entrance road. The road climbs steeply up the mesa. The Visitor Center is about 15 miles from US 160, and the cliff dwellings are a little more than 20 miles. This is not just an hour-long trip. Allow a day at least. If you are a history buff, you will want to spend much more time there.

THE MILLION DOLLAR HIGHWAY

This is a fine trip to take when you are anywhere in the Four Corners area. In fact, if you are going to hunt at the Bullion King Mine (Site 30), you will have no choice but to take the Million Dollar Highway.

The Million Dollar Highway (US 550) offers more spectacular scenery per mile than any other paved road in Colorado. It was built originally as a toll road for the freight traffic from the area's mines. Today, the modern paved highway runs from Ouray south through Silverton and on to Durango. The most dramatic stretch is the climb out of Ouray across a shelf cut from the solid rock wall. The road is two-lane blacktop, but there is no guardrail, and passengers have been known to arrive at the end of the shelf road noticeably paler than when they started.

Beyond the shelf road, the highway passes through the remains of the old town of Ironton and into a series of switchbacks to Red Mountain Pass. From the pass, the road winds down the mountain past the site of the town of Chattanooga and through a pretty valley into Silverton.

As the highway leaves Silverton, there are turnouts that offer panoramic views of the valley, Silverton, and the surrounding mountains. The climb continues past Molas Lake, over Molas Pass, on to Coal Bank Pass, and finally into Durango. There are turnouts all along the way, and the views are spectacular. If you are lucky enough to pass this way in the fall when the aspens are turning, you had better have a lot of film or extra digital memory cards.

PAWNEE BUTTES

An interesting side trip out of Fort Collins on CO 14 is to Pawnee Buttes, unusual landmarks in the middle of the Pawnee National Grasslands. Because of a top layer of sandstone and conglomerate, the twin formations have been able to resist the erosion that has taken place all around them. Consequently, they stand out starkly at more than 200 feet above the surrounding landscape in a largely barren prairie.

In 1907, mammal fossils from the Oligocene and Miocene Epochs were discovered at the buttes. Fossilized skeletons of more than a hundred land mammals have been recovered. Among the finds were camels, horses, and rhinoceroses.

Finding the site: By far the best way to find Pawnee Buttes is to make some local inquiries and get specific directions. There are a bazillion roads in the area and all are marked with county numbers. All of the intersections even have street signs. The trouble is that they don't seem to relate to anything. The roads are wide and smooth, but there are just too many of them. Some are marked with signs to Pawnee Buttes, and you could probably wander around and find them, but you might find Wyoming or Nebraska first. Be aware also that this is a very big county with no facilities, no water, or anything. Be sure you have a full tank of gas and plenty of drinking water before you venture out here.

PIKES PEAK

Even if you are not planning to do any rockhounding in the Pikes Peak area, you know that you cannot go home and face your friends and neighbors without having visited the top of the peak. It is only the twenty-eighth highest peak in the state, and the view from the top, while beautiful, is surpassed by the views from many other peaks and passes in Colorado. As Colorado peaks go, it is not even the most spectacular, but it is the most visited and probably the most famous mountain in the country. It is one of the few places where you can take your family sedan up to 14,000 feet over a fine graded road. If you wish, you can take the world-famous cog railroad to the top from Manitou Springs. Of course, you can walk or ride your bicycle, too. No matter how you do it, you are obligated to get to the top before you go home.

Finding the site: From the junction of I-25 and US 24 in Colorado Springs, go west on US 24 for 11.5 miles to the well-marked turnoff for the toll road. Inquire in Manitou Springs about the cog railroad.

ROCKY MOUNTAIN NATIONAL PARK

Several of the sites in this book put you so close to Rocky Mountain National Park that you have no excuse not to visit. The 417 square miles of the park straddle the Continental Divide and display Colorado mountain majesty at its finest. Eighty of the peaks in the park are more than 10,000 feet high and eighteen of those are more than 12,000 feet high. US 34, known in the park as Trail Ridge Road, generally follows the ridges and provides unsurpassed views. From climbing challenges, such as the 2,000-foot face of Longs Peak for the technical mountain climber, to a half-hour walk in a field of wildflowers, Rocky Mountain National Park has something for everyone. Three hundred miles of trails offer everything from a short walk to strenuous hikes. Young and old and all of us in between can enjoy the beauty of this land of high peaks, wildflowers, mountain lakes, wild animals, and serenity. Because of the tourist traffic, it may be necessary to walk a little to find that serenity, but it will be worth it. Fortunately for those of us who do crave peace and quiet, most of those who travel through the park have a rather short umbilical cord attached to their vehicle.

Finding the site: To reach the park from the east, take US 34 west from Loveland for about 30 miles to Estes Park. Follow the signs to the park entrance. From the southwest follow US 34 north from its junction with US 40 at Granby.

THE SPANISH PEAKS

When you have fulfilled your fossil hunting desires at Russell (Site 80), continue on US 160 over La Veta Pass and take the drive down CO 12 to the Spanish Peaks area. The peaks rise about 7,000 feet above the surrounding plains and mark the boundary between the Great Plains and the mountains to the west. They were, for a long time, a navigation point for early visitors to the area and were of religious significance to the nearby Indigenous tribes. The summer storms that gathered around the peaks were proof to these Indigenous people that the rain gods lived there.

The Spanish Peaks were formed when igneous rock was injected into the existing sedimentary rock. The igneous rock filled cracks and crevices in the sedimentary rock and formed volcanic dikes that radiate from the peaks. The softer sedimentary rock has eroded away and left the igneous dikes standing. More than 400 of these dikes have been identified, with some exceeding 100 feet in width. This forms some dramatic scenery that is well worth a side trip to view.

Finding the site: At about 15 miles east of La Veta Pass on US 160, CO 12 goes south toward the town of La Veta. From La Veta go south on CO 12 for 6.4 miles. The Spanish Peaks may be seen to the east, and the road passes several of the dikes, including the Devil's Staircase. Continue another 10.9 miles to Cucharas Pass. From the summit of the pass, take the Cordova Pass Scenic Drive toward Cordova Pass. There are good views of the Spanish Peaks and an interesting tunnel through one of the igneous dikes along the road. The road beyond the tunnel may be dangerous when wet, so you might want to backtrack to CO 12.

STONEWALL GAP

Stonewall Gap is a stream-eroded cut in a nearly vertical hogback that runs for miles in a north–south direction. The hogback was formed during the formation of the Culebra Range, and the tilt is so severe that what would normally be the sandstone cap is standing nearly vertical like a wall.

Finding the site: If you backtracked to CO 12 from your trip to the Spanish Peaks and would like to see Stonewall Gap, continue south on CO 12 for about 12 or 15 miles to Monument Lake. Check your odometer at Monument Lake and drive 4.3 miles south on CO 12 to where the highway passes through the gap.

WHEELER NATIONAL GEOLOGIC AREA

If you are in Creede (Site 49) and you have a four-wheel-drive vehicle, you may want to visit this unique geologic area. In the late 1800s, this was the second most visited tourist attraction in Colorado. Only Pikes Peak drew more visitors.

The area was named for Lieutenant George Montague Wheeler, who led an army surveying party through the southwest. In 1908, President Theodore Roosevelt designated the site as Wheeler National Monument. Unlike most parks and monuments, the increasing popularity of the automobile caused travel to the monument to dwindle and stop. The area was an 8-mile horseback ride from Creede, and in those days that was not thought to be a long ride. No road was ever built to the monument, however, and the automobiles of the day (or now for that matter) were not up to such a rough trip. In fact, the trip might be better done as a hike than a jeep trip. You will have to be a good hiker and in good shape, though, since the trip is 7 miles each way, and the altitude is more than 11,000 feet. If you decide to four-wheel it, be prepared for a rough, bumpy, and probably very muddy ride. Is it worth it? You will have to answer that.

The features in the monument are strangely eroded formations of compressed volcanic ash. There are crevices, spires, caves, and balanced rocks with names like The White Shrouded Ghosts, Phantom Ships, and Dante's Lost Souls. If you make the trip, allow plenty of time for exploring, and don't forget the camera and lots of film or memory cards.

Finding the site: From Creede drive 7.2 miles east on CO 149 to the junction of Rio Grande National FR 600. This is known locally as Pool Table Road. Take the road east for approximately 10 miles to the site of Hansen's Mill. A restroom marks the spot. This is where four-wheel drive becomes a necessity. The hiking trail forks left, and the jeep road goes to the right. You would be wise to inquire in Creede about the road condition and get a map of the area. The Rio Grande National Forest map is a good one, but you might get an even better one locally.

NORTHWESTERN COLORADO

1. Wolf Creek Agate

Agate at Wolf Creek.

Land type: Mountain meadow.
Elevation: 6,968 feet.
GPS: N40 22.719′ / W108 44.992′
Best season: Spring through fall.
Land manager: BLM.
Material: Agate and jasper.
Tools: Rock hammer and digging tools.
Vehicle: Any.
Accommodations: Motels, RV parking, and camping in Craig area; and camping in Dinosaur National Monument.
Special attraction: Dinosaur National Monument.
Finding the site: The Elk Springs area lies just north of US 40 at the southeast end of Dinosaur National Monument. From the town of Massadona, take US 40 east for 5.3 miles to the intersection of Moffat County Road 16. Turn north onto

CR 16 and proceed northwest for 14 miles to the intersection of CR 14. At the intersection, there is a pie-shaped area with CR 16 on one side, CR 14 on another, and a shortcut between the two forming the third side. Park in the center of the "pie."

Check hill east of Site 1.

Rockhounding

The whole expanse around the parking area contains agate and jasper. You will find good pieces on the hillside just to the east of the parking area. More agate has been reported along the banks of Wolf Creek, and there is agate for a mile or so to the north along CR 14. Most of the material we found is under fist size, but plenty big enough for cabochons. If your rockhounding desires run toward digging, you may well find some very nice large pieces.

Parked at Site 1.

Sites 1-2

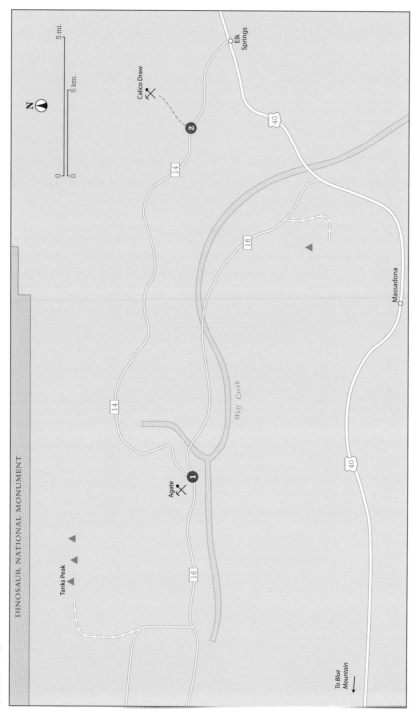

DINOSAUR NATIONAL MONUMENT

Tanks Peak

Agate

Calico Draw

Elk Springs

Massadona

Wolf Creek

To Blue Mountain

N

5 mi.

5 km.

2. Calico Draw

Dirt road leading to site.

See map on page 26.
Land type: Mountains.
Elevation: 6,700 feet.
GPS: N40 22.685′ / W108 31.331′
Best season: Spring through fall.
Land manager: BLM.
Material: Agate and jasper.
Tools: Rock hammer.
Vehicle: High-clearance.
Accommodations: Motels, RV parking, and camping in Craig area; and camping in Dinosaur National Monument.
Special attraction: Dinosaur National Monument.
Finding the site: At Elk Springs on US 40, take Moffat County Road 14 northwest for 4.6 miles. If you have passed the small rest area at Elk Springs,

you have gone too far. CR 14 starts just west of the rest area. Turn northeast onto the dirt track marked Calico Draw, where it intersects CR 14. Follow it through the cedars.

Rockhounding

There are scattered pieces of agate and jasper on both sides of the track. It gets a little rougher as you go, so just proceed until you have collected enough. We don't know just how far the track goes. Maybe you will find out.

Agate and jasper found at Calico Draw.

Watch for sign at turnoff.

3. Cross Mountain

Parking area at Cross Mountain.

Land type: Mountains.
Elevation: 5,709 feet.
GPS: N40 27.130' / W108 22.872'
Best season: Spring through fall.
Land manager: BLM.
Material: Agate and jasper.
Tools: Rock hammer.
Vehicle: Any.
Accommodations: Motels, RV parking, and camping in Craig area; and camping at Dinosaur National Monument.
Special attraction: Dinosaur National Monument.
Finding the site: On US 40, 16.1 miles west of Maybell, Twelve Mile Gulch Road heads northwest toward Dinosaur National Monument. If you are coming from the west, Twelve Mile Gulch Road is 7 miles east of Elk Springs. The road is paved and

is used as access to the east side of the monument. Proceed along this road for 3.9 miles to a road that exits to the right and leads a half mile or so to a parking area. The parking area is on the Yampa River, and you can find a little agate and jasper along the banks of the river. There is much better collecting about a quarter mile back toward Twelve Mile Gulch Road, where an unmarked track leads off to the east. The track is very rough and sandy, so if you don't have at least a high-clearance vehicle, park and walk.

Check this area for agate and jasper.

Rockhounding

You will find agate and jasper along both sides of the track.

Site 3

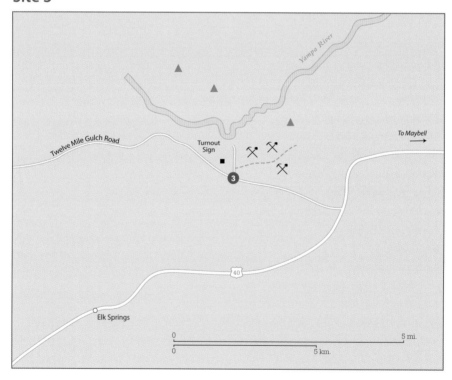

4. Douglas Mountain

Check washes in the area for agate.

Land type: Mountains.
Elevation: 5,744 feet.
GPS: N40 32.932' / W108 25.583'
Best season: Spring through fall.
Land manager: BLM.
Material: Agate.
Tools: Rock hammer.
Vehicle: Any.
Accommodations: Motels, RV parking, and camping in Craig area; and camping at Dinosaur National Monument.
Special attraction: Dinosaur National Monument.

Washes hold good agate pieces.

Finding the site: From the road to the parking area at Cross Mountain (Site 3), continue along Twelve Mile Gulch Road for 1.9 miles to the intersection with

Moffat County Road 25. Turn right onto CR 25 and go 7.9 miles to the intersection of CR 25 and CR 10. Take the left fork and cross the bridge. Turn to the left and drive along this track and look for little gullies running down to the river. There was a four-wheel drive recommended sign at the start of this road. We had a four-wheel drive, but I believe that any vehicle could easily make this trip. Of course, the weather was dry and sunny when we visited; we did see some spots that looked as though they could be big trouble if they were wet. If you make this trip in early spring or after a rain, you should make local inquiries about road conditions.

Rockhounding

Hunt in the gullies and along the sandy riverbank for small but nice pieces of agate. The material is not plentiful, but if you are patient and spend some time, you will be rewarded for your effort.

Site 4

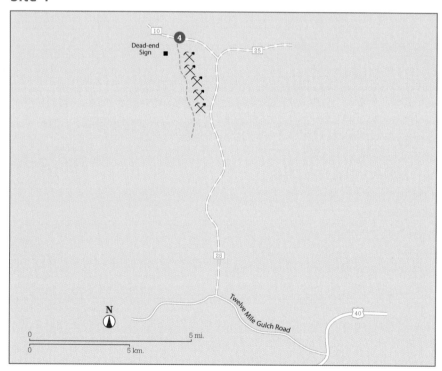

5. Troublesome Creek

Bad road but nice pieces of wood in the area.

Land type: Hills.
Elevation: 7,529 feet.
GPS: N40 06.370' / W106 16.712'
Best season: Spring through fall.
Land manager: BLM.
Material: Agate and petrified wood.
Tools: Rock hammer.
Vehicle: Any.
Accommodations: Motels, RV parking, and camping in Kremmling; and motels in Hot Sulphur Springs.
Special attraction: Rocky Mountain National Park.
Finding the site: From the eastern city limits sign in Kremmling, go 4 miles east on US 40 to Grand County Road 2. Take CR 2 north for 3.6 miles and park off the road.

Rockhounding

Hunt on the slopes and along the tops of the low hills to the east of the road for some nice pieces of black agate, black agatized wood, and specimen wood. The black agate makes nice specimens, but most are too porous for use in jewelry unless made into doublets or triplets.

While in this area, you might want to visit the Kremmling Cretaceous Ammonite Research Area about 10 miles north of Kremmling. This area covers 200 acres and in addition to a huge variety of marine fossils, has produced ammonites up to 2 feet in diameter. The area is protected and closed to collecting, but you can get permission to visit by contacting the BLM's Kremmling Resource Area office in Kremmling. Check Appendix C for the phone number. They will give you directions and may even be able to tell you where you can do some legal collecting.

Site 5

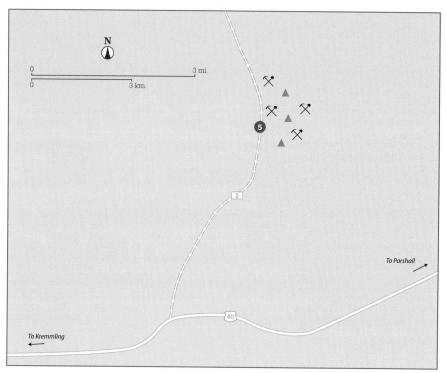

6. Green Mountain Reservoir

Site overlooking Green Mountain Reservoir.

Land type: Mountains.
Elevation: 8,104 feet.
GPS: N39 51.964' / W106 15.547'
Best season: Spring through fall.
Land manager: Arapaho National Forest.
Material: Fossils.
Tools: Small trowel and screen.
Vehicle: Any.
Accommodations: Motels in Kremmling and Dillon; and Forest Service campground at south end of reservoir.
Special attraction: Green Mountain Reservoir.
Finding the site: From Kremmling drive south on CO 9 for about 10 miles to Green Mountain Reservoir. If you are coming from Dillon, drive north on CO 9 for about 15 miles. Green Mountain Reservoir is about 5 miles long, and CO 9 parallels

it most of the way. Look for the long and very high black shale roadcuts. There are several places where you can park safely away from the traffic, but you may have to walk a ways to get to the collecting areas. If you hunt along the base of the high roadcuts, be extremely careful since the cuts are very steep and the material is loose. This is also a place to watch the children closely. The traffic moves fast and is closer than desired.

Rockhounding

Pelecypod and cephalopod fossils can be found in the high roadcuts near the south end of the reservoir along CO 9. We found small but nice examples on the southwest side of the highway, 1.5 miles northwest of the entrance to the Prairie Point Forest Campground. While we managed to get by with a rock hammer, a small trowel and a screen with about a quarter-inch mesh would be better. It will take some patience to find the best specimens.

Site 6

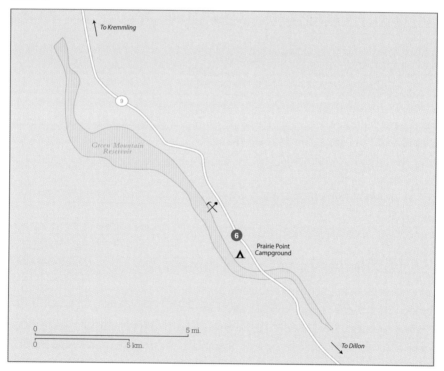

To Kremmling

9

Green Mountain
Reservoir

6

Prairie Point
Campground

0   5 mi.
0   5 km.

To Dillon

7. Rock Candy Mountain

When you see this cliff, you are at Rock Candy Mountain (Site 7).

Land type: Mountains.
Elevation: 5,616 feet.
GPS: N39 27.995' / W108 46.720'
Best season: Spring through fall.
Land manager: BLM.
Material: Fossils.
Tools: Rock hammer, chisels, and splitting tool.
Vehicle: Any.
Accommodations: Motels and campgrounds in Grand Junction area.
Special attractions: None.
Finding the site: Take I-70 about 16 miles west of Grand Junction to exit 15 at Loma. At Loma go north on CO 139 for 20.4 miles. At that point you will see a colorful cliff with yellow and red stripes on the west side of the road. There is a dirt turnoff where you can park just below the cliff. These are really clinker

beds, formed by heat from nearby coal beds, but the colors are so bright that we couldn't resist calling the area Rock Candy Mountain.

Rockhounding

Walk along the base of the cliff and look at the rubble carefully. You will find some of what others have left, which will give you an idea of what you are looking for. There is a lot of plant material in the shale-like layers. It is not like the delicate leaves at Douglas Pass (Site 8), but it is interesting and worth collecting nonetheless. When you know what you are looking for, start splitting some of the

Check these cliffs for fossils.

larger pieces. With a little time and some easy work, you will be rewarded with some nice samples for your collection.

Site 7

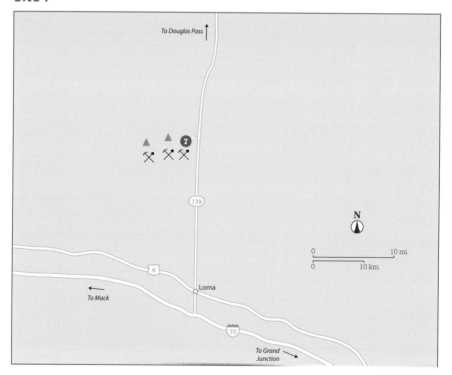

8. Douglas Pass

View from the top of Douglas Pass.

Land type: Mountaintop.
Elevation: 8,985 feet.
GPS: N39 58.192' / W108 45.709'
Best season: Spring through fall.
Land manager: BLM.
Material: Fossils.
Tools: Rock hammer, chisels, and splitting tools.
Vehicle: Any.
Accommodations: Motels, RV parking, and camping in Grand Junction area; and motels in Rangely.

This area holds plant fossil specimen.

Special attractions: None.
Finding the site: From I-70 about 16 miles west of Grand Junction, take exit 15 at Loma. At Loma follow CO 139 north for 33.6 miles to the top of Douglas Pass.

At the top take the unmarked road to the right. At 2.6 miles a road goes off to the right. Keep to the left. At 2.6 miles more another road goes off to the right. Keep to the left again. At 0.4 mile more you will arrive at the parking area for the Federal Aviation Administration's radar site. You can't miss the huge silver radar dome at the site. Park near the cut to the left of the dome.

Rockhounding

Look along the bottom of the cut at the rubble left by other fossil hunters. You will only find what other people have discarded or overlooked, but it will give you an idea of what you are looking for. The real prizes here are the large, delicately formed leaf imprints. Many have been found that measure more than 4 inches across. Don't be discouraged if you don't find any of those. There are plenty of little ones and they are a lot easier to get home. Take your hammer and splitting tools and go to work. This is a beautiful place, and you may find yourself looking at the view instead of splitting shale. Either way you can't lose.

Site 8

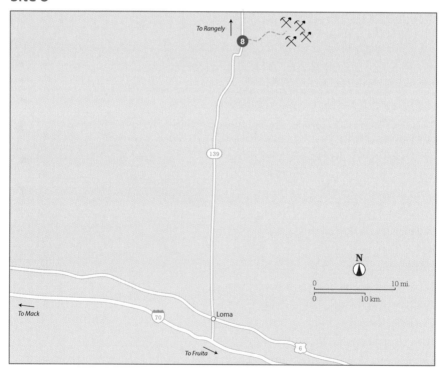

9. Rangely

Plant fossils can be found in these hillsides.

Land type: Mountains.
Elevation: 6,432 feet.
GPS: N39 44.543' / W108 47.719'
Best season: Spring through fall.
Land manager: BLM.
Material: Fossils.
Tools: Rock hammer, chisels, and splitting tool.
Vehicle: Any.
Accommodations: Motels, RV parking, and camping in Grand Junction area; motels in Rangely.
Special attractions: None.
Finding the site: Take I-70 about 16 miles west of Grand Junction to exit 15 at Loma. At Loma take CO 139 north for 33.6 miles to Douglas Pass. From the pass proceed another 13.6 miles. If you are coming from Rangely, travel 25.6 miles.

At this point there is a turnoff to the left to a clinker bed cliff similar to the one at Rock Candy Mountain (Site 7).

Rockhounding

The plant fossils here are similar to the ones at Rock Candy Mountain (Site 7). Search the rubble to find out what is there, find a likely spot, then use your hammer and chisel to break the rock and expose the treasures within.

If you are staying at Rangely, you might want to take a ride over toward Meeker on CO 64 to the Blacks Gulch fossil area. The area is off-limits to collecting, but is a fascinating spot that has been studied by paleontologists for many years and has yielded hundreds of fossilized bones. Check with the BLM office in Meeker (see Appendix C) for directions, information on what can be seen, and restrictions on collecting.

Site 9

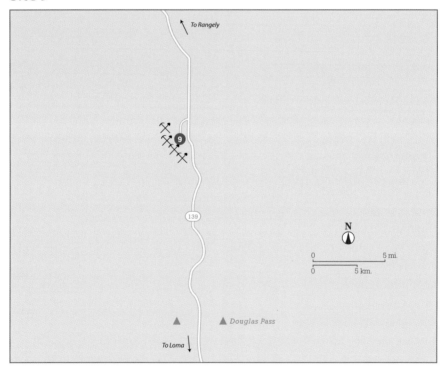

10. Gypsum

Selenite crystals are in this area by the side of the road.

Land type: Roadcut.
Elevation: 6,289 feet.
GPS: N39 39.242' / W106 57.837'
Best season: Spring through fall.
Land manager: Colorado Department of Transportation.
Material: Selenite crystals.
Tools: Rock hammer and splitting tool.
Vehicle: Any.
Accommodations: Motels in Eagle; and RV parking and camping at Sylvan Lake State Park near Eagle.
Special attractions: None.
Finding the site: The Gypsum site is approximately 25 miles east of Glenwood Springs just off I-70. Leave the freeway at exit 140, go north to the frontage road, and turn west. Proceed 0.5 mile and park.

Rockhounding

Hunt in the gray and black ash of the roadcut. This area has been picked over for years now and we did not find too many crystals here. This is such an easy site to get to that you can stop for a while even if you are just passing by on I-70. There is virtually no traffic on the frontage road, so the kids can have fun here, too.

Selenite crystals in roadcut at Gypsum site.

Sites 10-11

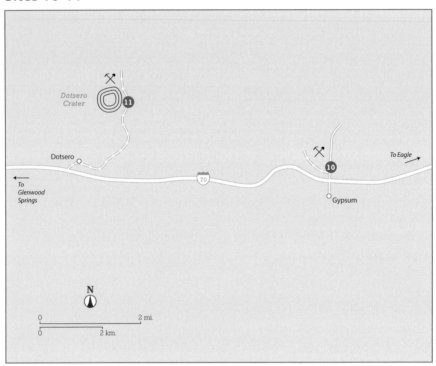

11. Dotsero

Edge of the volcanic crater at Dotsero.

See map on page 44.
Land type: Mountains.
Elevation: 7,063 feet.
GPS: N39 39.541' / W107 01.989'
Best season: Spring through fall.
Land manager: BLM and private.
Material: Volcanic specimens.
Tools: None.
Vehicle: High-clearance or four-wheel drive.
Accommodations: Motels in Eagle; and RV parking and camping at Sylvan Lake State Park near Eagle.
Special attraction: Volcanic crater.
Finding the site: Dotsero is 18 miles east of Glenwood Springs on I-70. Leave the freeway at exit 133 and go north to the unmarked frontage road heading east. Proceed along this road about 0.5 mile to the mobile home area. Turn left

and almost immediately back to the right. Follow this twisting, climbing road for 1.8 miles to the rim of the volcano. You will see the crater on your left before you reach the rim. Park in the pullout and walk to the edge for a great view of the crater. Continue up the road to the top of the crater rim. The area at the top is being worked and is private land or under claim, so be sure to get permission before you do any searching in the tailings.

Rockhounding

When we (Gary and Sally Warren) were there in 2015, this volcano site had been left to nature. We did talk with a gentleman who was out walking his dog in this area and he told us that they use to find good quartz crystals on the north side of the volcano; so, you might want to work your way over and see what you can find. The north side is part of BLM land. It is a little hard to get to, but there should be more samples there because few people want to hike there. There is nothing here for the lapidary, but if you would like to have bits of volcanic rock in your collection, this is your spot.

There are two little bits of trivia that any visitor to Dotsero should know. First, the most recent eruption of the volcano was a little more than 4,000 years ago and qualifies Dotsero as Colorado's youngest volcano. Second, the name Dotsero is said to have come from early cartographers who used the area in their mapping as "Dot Zero."

The Dotsero volcanic crater.

12. Wolcott

This hillside holds small fossils and some calcite crystals.

Land type: Roadcut.
Elevation: 7,172 feet.
GPS: N39 43.376' / W106 40.705'
Best season: Spring through fall.
Land manager: Colorado Department of Transportation.
Material: Fossils.
Tools: Rock hammer, chisels, and splitting tool.
Vehicle: Any.
Accommodations: Motels in Eagle; and RV parking and camping at Sylvan State Park near Eagle.
Special attractions: None.
Finding the site: Leave I-70 at exit 157 about 9 miles east of Eagle. Proceed north on CO 131 for 2.1 miles. At this point, there is a road going off to the right to the Eagle County landfill. Turn onto the road and park in the wide area on the north side.

Rockhounding

Hunt for small pelecypod fossils in the gray shale hill north of the landfill road and in the roadcut on CO 131. The fossils are fragile, so be sure to have something to transport them in for the trip home. Some of the seams in the shale contain calcite crystals, so keep your eyes peeled.

Fossils and calcite crystals are in this area.

Site 12

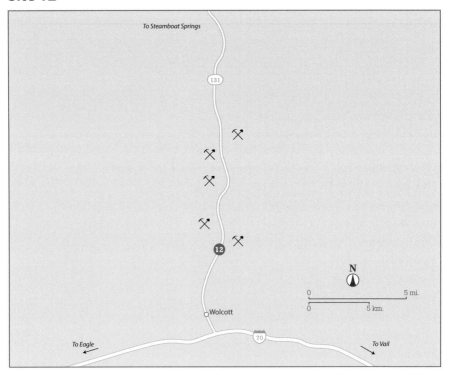

13. Delaney Butte

Check the washes in the area for fossils.

Land type: High valley.
Elevation: 8,145 feet.
GPS: N40 41.731' / W106 27.872'
Best season: Spring through fall.
Land manager: Colorado Division of Wildlife.
Material: Fossils.
Tools: Rock hammer, chisels, and splitting tool.
Vehicle: Any.
Accommodations: Motels and camping in Steamboat Springs; and camping in Walden area.
Special attractions: Wildlife refuge and fishing.
Finding the site: This trip begins at Walden, which is about 100 miles west of Fort Collins and about 60 miles north of Steamboat Springs. From the intersection of CO 125 and CO 14 in Walden, take CO 14 southwest for 0.6 mile to Jackson County Road 12W. Follow CR 12W for 5.3 miles. At this point, the road forks. Take the left

fork (Jackson County Road 18) for 4.5 miles to another fork. Follow the right fork that runs between the butte and the lake. At 1 mile, you will come to a cattle guard. Turn around and go back 0.2 mile. Park and walk up the little wash toward the butte. This area has been made into a state park and most assuredly the roads have changed since 1995. We could not exactly find the right wash, but in checking the surrounding area, we did find some clam fossils, so check in the area of where the GPS reading was taken and go from there.

The directions to this site sound a bit complicated, but the land out here is flat, and the butte is visible for miles before you get to it. All of the roads are well marked to Delaney Butte.

Rockhounding

Nice little pelecypod fossils are found all along this wash. Many are exposed, but the shale splits very easily. A little work will net you some treasures.

Fluorite crystals are reported on top of the butte, but we could not find a jeep road to the top, and the hike was too lengthy for the time available. If you have the time, give it a try.

Site 13

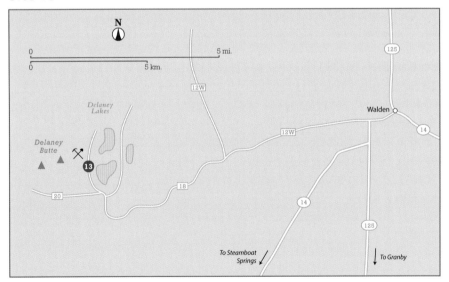

14. Rabbit Valley

Agate and small, sand-filled iron balls are in this area by the side of the road.

Land type: Low hills.
Elevation: 4,762 feet.
GPS: N39 11.520′ / W109 01.691′
Best season: Spring through fall.
Land manager: BLM.
Material: Iron concretions, agate, and chalcedony.
Tools: Rock hammer.
Vehicle: Any.
Accommodations: Motels, hotels, RV parking, and campgrounds in Grand Junction.
Special attraction: Rabbit Valley Research Natural Area.
Finding the site: Follow I-70 west from Grand Junction for 28 miles to the well-marked Rabbit Valley turnoff. If you are traveling east from Utah, the turnoff is just 1 mile east of the Utah/Colorado state line. Stay to the north of the freeway and head toward the Trails Thru Time area. Before you go into the Trails Thru Time,

make a left turn and you will see a road that goes up the hill. Pull up the hill and find a place to park and start looking.

Rockhounding

This is a site right next to the freeway, but one that hasn't been rock-hounded out. There are nice, though small, pieces of agate and chalcedony scattered all over within a few yards of the dirt road shown on the map. Most interesting, though, are the sand-filled iron balls in the boulders on the hillside. You can pick them out of the matrix with a little careful rock hammer work, or you can just look around for the ones that have weathered out and are lying on the ground just waiting for you to pick them up and give them a good home.

If you have a little energy left after collecting, you might want to try the 1.5-mile walk at the Rabbit Valley Research Natural Area. This is a well-visited dinosaur quarry with a self-guided tour.

Site 14

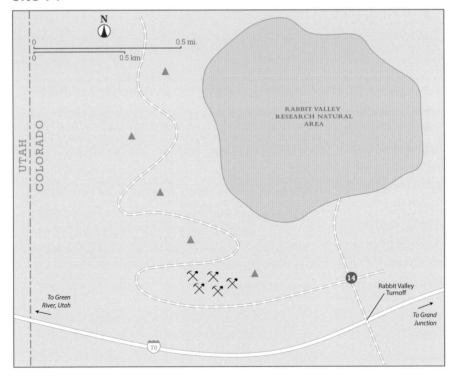

NORTHEASTERN COLORADO

15. Genessee Dike

A large piece of white feldspar next to the parking area of Genessee Dike (Site 15).

Land type: Roadcut.
Elevation: 7,188 feet.
GPS: N39 44.363' / W105 25.628'
Best season: Spring through fall.
Land manager: Colorado Department of Transportation.
Material: Feldspar, mica, and quartz.
Tools: Rock hammer.
Vehicle: Any.
Accommodations: Motels, RV parking, and camping in Idaho Springs area.
Special attractions: Lookout Mountain and Buffalo Bill's Grave.
Finding the site: Go west of Denver on I-70 to exit 256. Turn west on US 40 and continue for 0.6 mile. Park on the left side of the highway in the wide pullout. Hunt in the large roadcut just across the highway.

Rockhounding

Not only is this a very old collecting site, but it is also right on US 40, just a stone's throw (no pun intended) from I-70. Considering its proximity to thousands of cars a day, there is a surprising amount of material still to be collected. We found very nice white feldspar with gray quartz crystals and black biotite mica, which make great displays. Garnet and epidote have also been reported here, but we didn't find any. If you have a screen, work on the leftovers at the foot of the cut. It is a pretty good bet that you will find some small crystals for micromounting.

There is a nice wide parking area just across from the cut, where the GPS reading was taken, but the cut itself is very close to a busy highway. Don't collect here with small children.

Site 15

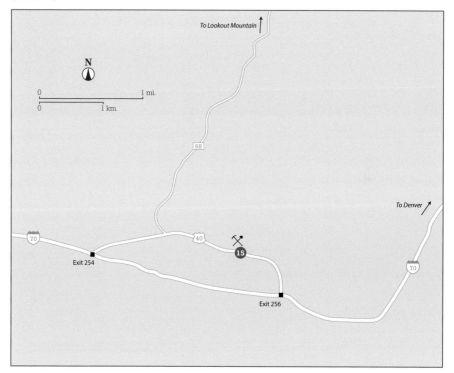

16. Boulder

A major highway runs next to this site.

Land type: Roadcut.
Elevation: 5,521 feet.
GPS: N40 06.210' / W105 16.920'
Best season: Spring through fall.
Land manager: Colorado Department of Transportation.
Material: Fossils.
Tools: Rock hammer and splitting tool.
Vehicle: Any.
Accommodations: Motels, RV parking, and camping in Boulder.
Special attraction: Colorado School of Mines Geology Museum at Golden.
Finding the site: From the intersection of US 36 and CO 7 north of Boulder, go north on US 36 for 2.5 miles to the Neva Road turnoff. Park as far off the highway as possible.

Rockhounding

Hunt in the roadcut on the west side of US 36 just north of the turnoff. There is a large pull off on US 36 just past the turnoff at Neva Road. Pelecypod fossils are found in the shale along and on top of the cut. Fossils have been reported in many of the roadcuts on US 36 between Boulder and Lyons, but this is the only cut where we had

Small fossils are found in shale in this area.

any luck. The fossils are small, and some are not too well defined, but it is an easy site to get to and worth a look if you are in the area. It should be noted, though, that the cut is very close to a busy highway. Don't collect here with the kids.

Site 16

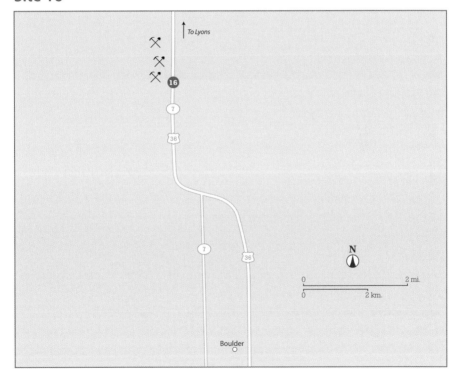

17. Golden Gate Canyon

Mica shines from the roadcuts.

Land type: Mountains and roadcuts.
Elevation: 7,531 feet.
GPS: N39 47.301' / W105 20.830'
Best season: Spring through fall.
Land manager: Colorado Department of Transportation.
Material: Feldspar, mica, and black tourmaline.
Tools: Rock hammer.
Vehicle: Any.
Accommodations: Motels, RV parking, and camping in Golden Gate Canyon; and RV parking and camping in Nederland area.
Special attraction: Golden Gate Canyon State Park.
Finding the site: From the intersection of US 6, CO 93, and CO 58 in Golden, drive north on CO 93 for 1.4 miles to the intersection of the Golden Gate Canyon Road (CO 46). Turn northwest onto Golden Gate Canyon Road and travel approximately 4 miles. From this point on, you will see flashes of mica in the roadcuts. Pull over

wherever you can and park. Search all of the cuts along the way. When you have gone a total of 7.9 miles from the CO 93 intersection, you will come to a road going left. This is the Robinson Hill Road. Turn onto it and park off the shoulder next to the high roadcut. Hunt in the cut. The Golden Gate Canyon Road is so full of mica that it looks like someone has taken a silver spray paint can and used it all over the cuts in the road. This is a very interesting area to see and view even if you are not rock hunting.

Rockhounding

Feldspar and mica are in great abundance all along Golden Gate Canyon Road. Pick those outcroppings that have an area to pull out and park, since this is a fairly busy road and the cuts are close to the traffic. There is a nice pullout at the Robinson Hill Road site, and there is plenty of room to collect. Look for the light-colored material with the flecks of black tourmaline in them. We also found some light pink feldspar with gray quartz crystals, which makes a very nice cabinet specimen.

Site 17

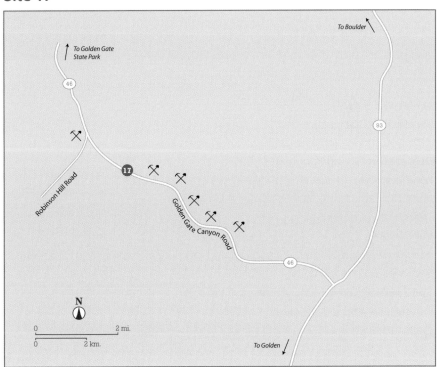

18. Sugarloaf Road

Watch for this guard on Sugarloaf Road (Site 18).

Land type: Mountains.
Elevation: 7,847 feet.
GPS: N40 10.195' / W105 24.368'
Best season: Spring through fall.
Land manager: Roosevelt National Forest.
Material: Biotite mica, white feldspar, and quartzite.
Tools: Rock hammer.
Vehicle: Any.
Accommodations: Motels, RV parking, and camping in Boulder; and RV parking and camping in Nederland.
Special attractions: Many old mines in the area.
Finding the site: This trip begins in Nederland, which is 14 miles west of Boulder, at the intersection of CO 119 and CO 72. From the intersection, go north on CO 72 for 3.1 miles and turn right onto Sugarloaf Road. Go 4.2 miles to Old Town

Site Road and turn and park in the parking area there. The tailings pile is now in a fenced area with a large camel guarding it! There are plenty of specimens in and around the area.

Rockhounding

On this large tailings pile, you might find schist with biotite mica, white feldspar, and some tiny red garnets. There is also quite a bit of a greenish quartzite.

White feldspar and quartzite.

Site 18

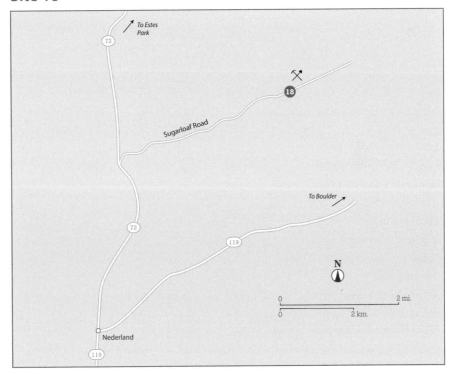

19. Jamestown

Feldspar, mica, and quartz line these cliffs.

Land type: Mountains.
Elevation: 6,714 feet.
GPS: N40 06.489' / W105 22.363'
Best season: Spring through fall.
Land manager: Boulder County Road Department.
Material: Feldspar, mica, quartz, and fluorite.
Tools: Rock hammer.
Vehicle: Any.
Accommodations: Motels, RV parking, and camping in Boulder; and national forest campgrounds in Nederland.
Special attraction: Golden Gate Canyon State Park.
Finding the site: From Lyons proceed southwest on CO 7 for 14 miles to CO 72. Go south on CO 72 for 5.7 miles. Turn west onto Boulder County Road 94. Proceed 5.4 miles and park on the wide shoulder on the north side of the road.

Rockhounding

In 8.3 miles, you should be opposite the Jamestown Post Office. From just east of the post office for a mile or so, the cliffs on the north side of the road have a lot of feldspar, quartz, and mica. They also produce some nice igneous granite with biotite mica, white feldspar, and gray quartz. There are several spots to pull off and park. With a little searching and a little work, you will come up with some fine samples.

There are many old mines in the Jamestown area, but most are under private claim. Check in town to see if any are open to collecting. If you can get permission to collect, you will be able to pick up some very nice fluorite specimens.

Site 19

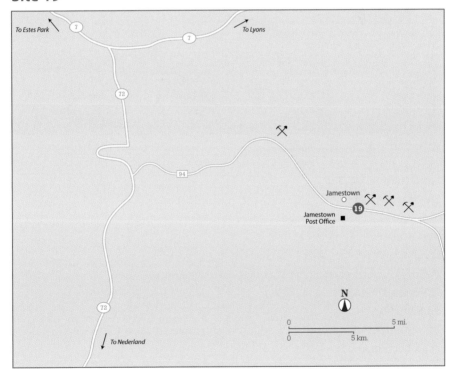

20. Crystal Mountain

Mica and beryl are found in this area.

Land type: Mountains.
Elevation: 8,546 feet.
GPS: N40 32.720' / W105 24.783'
Best season: Spring through fall.
Land manager: Roosevelt National Forest.
Material: Quartz crystals, feldspar, and muscovite mica.
Tools: Rock hammer.
Vehicle: Any.
Accommodations: Motels, RV parking, and camping in Loveland area; and motels in Fort Collins.
Special attraction: Rocky Mountain National Park.
Finding the site: From the intersection of US 287 and US 34 in Loveland, go west on US 34 for about 7 miles. At this point, take Larimer County Road 38E north for 5.3 miles to Masonville. From Masonville, go north on CR 27 for 10.9 miles to CR 44H. Follow CR 44H west for 8.5 miles to the intersection of Crystal Mountain

Road. Go south for 2.5 miles to a three-way fork. This will be as far as you can go as all roads are fenced off from this point. There are several places to pull in and park off the road. This area is now a large area for private homes so make sure that you are not on private land when hunting.

Rockhounding

You can start your search by breaking up the boulders on both sides of the road. This area is known for beryl and chrysoberyl.

When you tire of boulder bashing, go back up Crystal Mountain Road about 0.2 mile to the top of a small rise. A bermed-off track to the left leads to a big muscovite outcropping. There are large and pretty books of mica in the diggings. Green chrysoberyl often occurs along with these books, so spend a little time here. You might get lucky.

There are lots of old mines in this area, but many have had their access roads bermed off. Keep your eyes peeled for these old roads and explore them when you find them.

Site 20

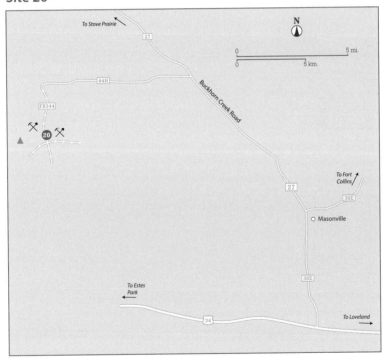

21. Owl Canyon

The small cave in the center of the photo is where the seam of calcite crystals can be found.

Land type: Hills.
Elevation: 5,782 feet.
GPS: N40 45.778' / W105 10.855'
Best season: Spring through fall.
Land manger: Private.
Material: Alabaster, calcite, and satin spar.
Tools: Rock hammer.
Vehicle: Any.
Accommodations: Motels, RV parking, and camping in Loveland area; motels in Fort Collins.
Special attraction: Colorado Lien Company limestone plant.
Finding the site: From Colorado State College on College Avenue (US 287) in Fort Collins, drive north on US 287 for 18.6 miles. You will come to Owl Canyon Road. Continue on for 0.5 mile where you will come to a large pullout where the GPS reading was taken.

Rockhounding

At the wide parking area, an old road used to turn off here, but it is fenced and blocked. Just inside the fenced area is a seam of calcite crystals about 10 or 15 feet up the cliff. We don't know the status of the land inside the fence. It may belong to the Colorado Department of Transportation, or it may be private land. Again, inquire at one of the nearby houses. The seam of calcite

A friend at the site in Owl Canyon.

looks as though everyone in the western United States has hunted there, so evidently no one cares about rockhounds taking the crystals. Remember, though, you should find out who owns it before you cross the fence.

Site 21

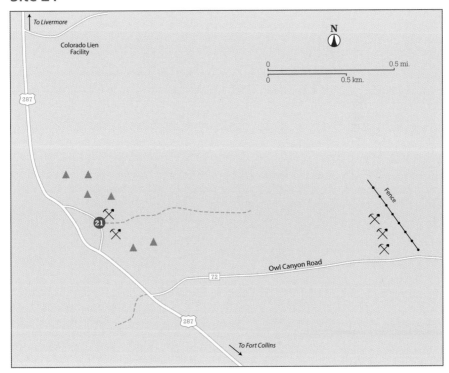

SOUTHWESTERN COLORADO

22. Opal Hill

This area is the site for common opal; walk through the gate and start hunting.

Land type: Hills.
Elevation: 4,557 feet.
GPS: N39 08.504' / W108 45.386'
Best season: Spring through fall.
Land manager: BLM.
Material: Common opal, jasper, and opalized wood.
Tools: Rock hammer.
Vehicle: Any.
Accommodations: Motels, RV parking, and camping in Grand Junction area.
Special attraction: Colorado National Monument.
Finding the site: From the intersection of I-70 and CO 340 at Fruita, just west of Grand Junction, take CO 340 south for 1.4 miles to Kingsview Road. Go west on Kingsview Road for 0.6 mile to Horsethief Canyon Road. Turn left on Horsethief Canyon Road and go a tenth of a mile. Turn right onto a gravel road that leads

around Opal Hill. As you get on the south side of Opal Hill, there is a parking area and an opening in the fence from where you can walk on up to Opal Hill.

Rockhounding

Hunt in all of the little gullies at the base of the hills. There is plenty of common opal, jasper, and petrified wood. This is an old rockhunt-

Opal Hill Site 22.

ing area and has been well picked over. Don't be discouraged, though; you will find good material. The farther you get from the road, the more you will find.

Site 22

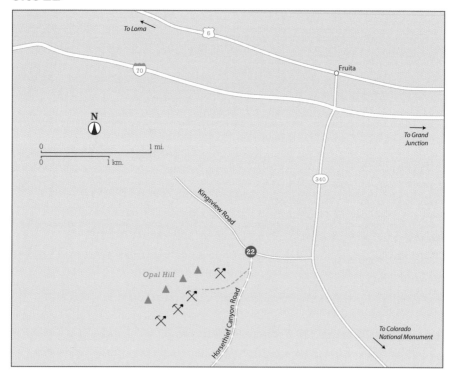

23. Piñon Mesa

This area is a great place to hunt for agate, jasper, and petrified wood.

Land type: High mesa.
Elevation: 7,250 feet.
GPS: N38 56.725' / W108 44.148'
Best season: Spring through fall.
Land manager: BLM.
Material: Agate, jasper, and petrified wood.
Tools: Rock hammer.
Vehicle: Any.
Accommodations: Motels, RV parking, and camping in Grand Junction; and campground in Colorado National Monument.
Special attraction: Colorado National Monument.
Finding the site: This trip begins at Glade Park, which is near the southwestern corner of the Colorado National Monument. Glade Park can be reached from

either the east or west entrance to the monument. From the west entrance, follow the road through the monument for about 11 miles to the West Glade Park Road. Proceed south on this road for 5 miles to Glade Park. From the east entrance, drive 4 miles to the East Glade Park Road (Mesa County Road DS). Follow this road for about 6 miles to Glade Park. At Glade Park, drive south on CR 16.5S for 3.5 miles. At this point, the road begins to climb toward Piñon Mesa. From here, the collecting area extends for almost 20 miles. The GPS site was taken at this point.

Rockhounding

Hunt on the flats and in all of the little gullies. If you have a high-clearance vehicle or four-wheel drive, explore all of the dirt tracks leading off into the trees. There is material in the areas under the trees, but the thick layer of pine needles makes for a lot of work. Look for clear areas first. This is a big area and will take some time to cover, but if you are patient, you will find enough nice agate, jasper, and petrified wood to make your efforts worthwhile.

Since you have to travel through part of the Colorado National Monument just to get to Piñon Mesa, you owe it to yourself to spend some time in this geologic wonder. The upper reaches of the monument tower is 2,000 feet above the Colorado River in the Grand Valley. The monument is a part of the Colorado Plateau, which also includes Grand Canyon and Arches National Park. Even if you only have time to take the 23-mile Rim Rock Drive through the monument, you will be rewarded with breathtaking views of the val-ley below and of deep can-yons and multicolored rock sculptures. If you have the time and energy, there are miles of hiking trails from a quarter-mile to 8.5 miles.

So here we have it: agate, jasper, petrified wood, hiking, unsurpassed scenery, picnic areas, and a camp-ground. Grab the hammers and the rock bags and get going.

Road to Piñon Mesa Site.

Site 23

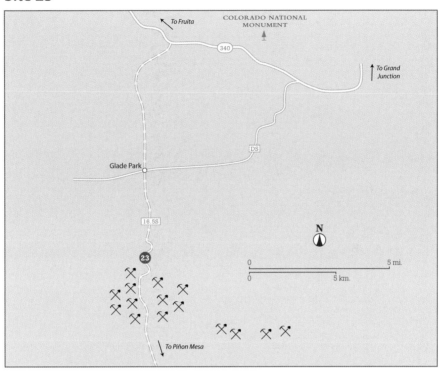

Nice pieces of agate are found in this area.

24. Whitewater

Cross the cattle guard and park here for Whitewater (Site 24).

Land type: Hills.
Elevation: 4,825 feet.
GPS: N38 56.733' / W108 24.364'
Best season: Spring through fall.
Land manager: BLM.
Material: Geodes.
Tools: Rock hammer.
Vehicle: Any.
Accommodations: Motels, RV parking, and camping (public and private) in Grand Junction area.
Special attraction: Colorado National Monument.
Finding the site: Whitewater is about 10 miles south of Grand Junction on US 50. From Whitewater, go south on US 50 for 1.3 miles. From here, the highway parallels gray shale cliffs to the east for nearly 10 miles. Between 3 and 3.5 miles

from Whitewater, there is a pull-off spot and a gate through the highway fence. You can park on the highway side of the fence or go through the gate and park on the flat at the foot of the slope. This is a difficult site to gain access to because the highway fence is so close to the road that there is no place to park. We strongly recommend using the gate.

Rockhounding

You will find pieces of geodes all the way up the slope to the cliffs on the east. If you want whole geodes, you will have to get high up on the cliffs where they originate. The geodes are generally filled with brownish calcite crystals, and some of them are a foot or so in diameter. They are not the most beautiful specimens in the world, but everyone should have one or two, shouldn't they?

Site 24

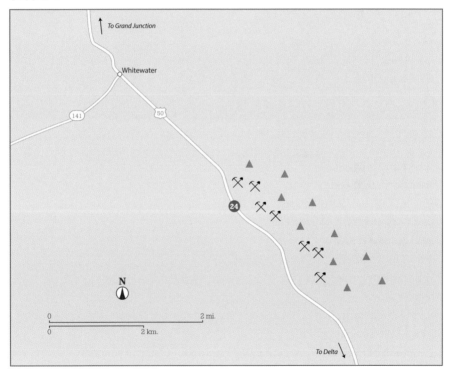

25. Copper Creek

Agate and pink feldspar can be found in this area.

Land type: Mountains.
Elevation: 6,260 feet.
GPS: N38 51.287′ / W108 31.892′
Best season: Spring through fall.
Land manager: BLM.
Material: Feldspar, mica, and amethyst.
Tools: Rock hammer.
Vehicle: Any.
Accommodations: Motels, RV parking, and camping in the Grand Junction area.
Special attractions: None.
Finding the site: From Whitewater on US 50 south of Grand Junction, take CO 141 southwest for just over 11 miles. At this point, you will cross a small bridge and will see a parking area off the road to your right. Pull into the parking area and hike up the remains of the old mine road to the north.

Rockhounding

This is part of the old Copper Creek Mining District, but the real prize here is amethyst. We think the mine at the end of the road is the Amethyst Queen, but are not sure. If there are "no tres-passing" signs, don't despair. There is a lot of nice collecting material all along the road outside the posted area. We found good pieces of pink feldspar with mica, which make nice cabinet speci-

Copper Creek mining area.

mens. We found a nice solid piece of black agate with white pattern, which looks very much like the agate at Troublesome Creek (Site 5). We also picked up a nice little piece of banded chalcedony. Maybe there are some relatives still there. We hope you find grandpa.

Site 25

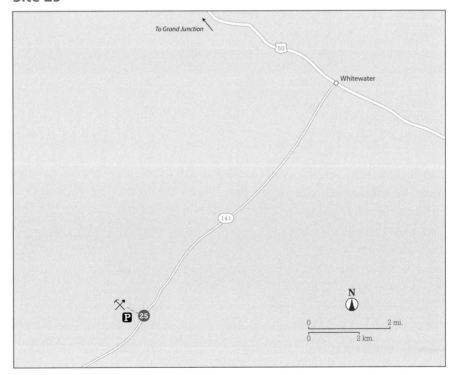

26. Gateway

Alabaster and barite can be found in this area.

Land type: Mountains.
Elevation: 4,794 feet.
GPS: N38 37.920' / W108 57.030'
Best season: Spring through fall.
Land manager: BLM.
Material: Barite and alabaster.
Tools: Rock hammer.
Vehicle: Any.
Accommodations: Motels, RV parking, and camping in Grand Junction area.
Special attractions: Old uranium mines near Naturita.
Finding the site: From the intersection of US 50 and CO 141 south of Grand Junction, go southwest on CO 141 for 42.6 miles to the Gateway store. This store is now closed but the building is still standing. From the store, proceed another 4.3 miles. At this point, you will see a hill with a roadcut on the west side of the road. Drive 0.2 mile farther and park at the pullout. At the end of the pullout is a gate

with a private property sign on it. Walk back to the hill, cross the fence, and walk back toward the parking place. The barite you are looking for is due west of a spot 0.1 mile north of the parking place.

Rockhounding

White barite is found in big chunks at the head of a caved-in mine. More barite is reported about 1 mile north of the roadcut and due west against the cliff. We didn't try this spot, but it looked promising.

The old Alabaster Box Mine is 1.1 miles south of the roadcut on a hillside to the west. It is easily seen from the road, but at the time we were there, it was posted to keep people out. Check on the status when you visit. There are some outcroppings that look like alabaster in the cliff north of the mine on BLM land, which might be worth checking out if you crave alabaster.

The Alabaster Box provided material for a lot of vases and urns. That in itself is not particularly interesting, but the mining method is. Instead of digging or blasting chunks of the material and then cutting them to size, the operator cut cores out of the cliff, then turned the cylinders on a lathe. The cliffs of alabaster looked like a giant honeycomb.

Site 26

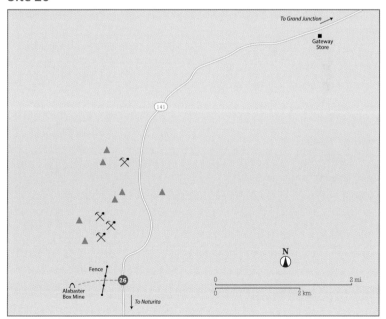

27. Ouray Mines

Views are great in this part of Colorado—you are entering the high country.

Land type: Mountains.
Elevation: 7,760 feet at Ouray; mines range up to over 12,000 feet.
Elevation at GPS site: 9,483 feet.
GPS: N37 58.538' / W107 44.090'
Best season: Summer.
Land manager: Uncompahgre National Forest and private.
Material: Mineral specimens.
Tools: Rock hammer and small digging tools.
Vehicle: Any to four-wheel drive.
Accommodations: Motels, RV parking, and camping (public and private) in Ouray area.
Special attractions: Historic town of Ouray and Million Dollar Highway.
Finding the site: On the south end of Ouray, turn right onto Campbird Road and then left as you start up the canyon. Follow this road for 4.7 miles to the first mine where the GPS was taken for this site. The best way to get started is to make local

inquiries or buy one of the many books available in Ouray listing the hundreds of mines in the area. As with all such areas, you will have better luck with four-wheel drive or hoofing it. If you can drive there in the family sedan, you can bet that a bazillion others have, too. Almost every jeep road in the area will take you to a spot worth exploring.

Rockhounding

The Ouray area is truly a fascinating place. If you are an old mine buff, this is your spot. Within a 10-mile radius of the town of Ouray are over 10,000 mine shafts, tunnels, and prospect holes. While some are on private property, some are posted claims, and some just yield nothing worth looking at, there are more awaiting your inspection than you will live long enough to explore.

Perhaps the most famous of the Ouray area mines is the huge Camp Bird Mine. The story of the Camp Bird is one of those tales of success that makes us all wonder why our grandparents were hanging around the cracker barrel in Omaha in 1895 instead of out looking for gold. It was in that year that a self-taught geologist by the name of Thomas Walsh began looking for some ore to use as flux in his small smelter in Ouray. With the aid of an old miner in the area, he found samples from some diggings high up in Imogene Basin. It didn't take him long to realize that the ore was a tellurium with a gold content worth $3,000 a ton. He began to buy out the old claims and eventually owned most of the claims in the basin. This complex of claims became the Camp Bird Mine, which, between 1896 and 1910, produced over $26 million in gold. So wealthy was this mine that at one time Thomas Walsh was able to buy his daughter the Hope Diamond.

It wasn't the same as the Hope Diamond, but some years ago, Joe Reidhead found a double-fist-sized chunk of amethyst-tinged quartz with a big vein of pyrite running right through the middle. This beauty was on a mine dump high up above the Camp Bird just off the jeep road over Imogene Pass. Maybe some of that rock's relatives are waiting for you.

Ouray mines.

Site 27

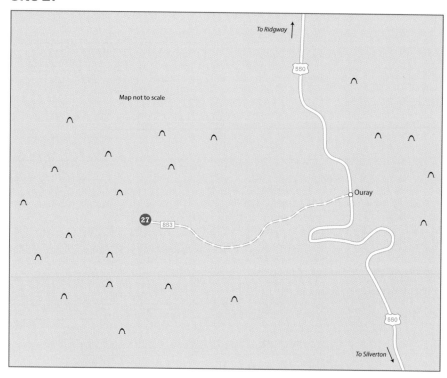

Lower Camp Bird Mining Area information sign.

28. Señorita Mine

The view from the Señorita Mine.

Land Type: Mountains.
Elevation: 6,363 feet.
GPS: N38 04.876' / W107 41.136'
Best season: Spring through fall.
Land manager: Uncompahgre National Forest.
Material: Malachite and azurite.
Tools: Rock hammer.
Vehicle: Any.
Accommodations: Motels, RV parking, and camping (public and private) in Ouray area.
Special attractions: Ouray mining district and historic town of Ouray.
Finding the site: From the northern edge of Ouray, go north on US 550 for 1.7 miles to Dexter Creek Road, CR14, which is clearly marked. Proceed up Dexter Creek Road. At 0.9 mile from US 550, you will come to a fork. The right fork goes to the Bachelor Mine; the left fork goes to the Señorita Mine. At 1.9 miles from US

550, a sign announces you are entering the Uncompahgre National Forest. Finally at 2.6 miles from US 550, you will come to a sharp right turn. Park on the outside of the turn and walk up the old road to the south. The GPS was taken at this point. In a hundred yards or so, you will reach the dumps of the Señorita Mine.

Rockhounding

Specimens of malachite and azurite are all over the dumps. Much of it is very colorful, but it is only a surface coating. The material is great for the sample collection, but not good for jewelry.

Site 28

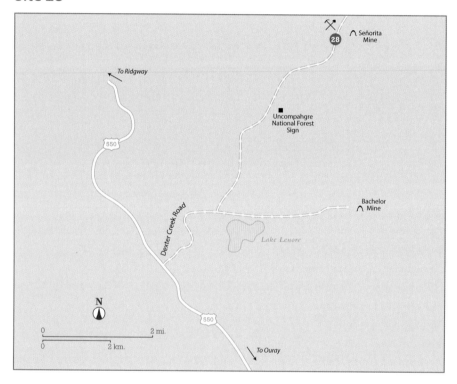

29. Bullion King Mine

Red Mountain Pass—note the elevation.

Land type: Mountains.
Elevation: 10,940 feet.
GPS: N37 53.454' / W107 43.328'
Best season: Late spring through early fall.
Land manager: Uncompahgre National Forest.
Material: Limonite pseudomorphs after pyrite.
Tools: Rock hammer and small digging tools.
Vehicle: Four-wheel drive.
Accommodations: Motels, RV parking, and camping in Ouray and Silverton areas.
Special attraction: Red Mountain Mining District.
Finding the site: The trip to the Bullion King Mine begins just south of Red Mountain Pass on the Million Dollar Highway (US 550). From the sign at the turnout at Red Mountain Pass, go south on US 550 for 0.7 mile. At this point, the unmarked jeep road to the Bullion King heads west. Follow this road for about 2 miles to the mine. The road crosses a small creek and turns left across the Bullion King tailings,

and it is impossible to miss. If you are new to this type of mountain driving, you may feel like you have gone 200 miles, but you haven't. The road to the mine is a typical Colorado jeep road. It is not particularly dangerous, and there are not many of those 1,000-foot drop-offs, but there are a few spots that will scare the novice. An experienced driver could make this with a high-clearance, two-wheel-drive vehicle, but four-wheel drive is preferred. If you rent a jeep for the trip, inquire about the road conditions from the rental agency before you start. When we were there in June 2015, the road was still impassable with snow drifts and we were not able to make it into the mine. We went as far as we could on the dirt/gravel road and then took the GPS reading. If we haven't scared you off, then you are in for both a scenic and rockhounding experience you won't soon forget. The scenery rivals that of Switzerland, and the rockhounding is for a relatively unique material. There is a site on Google called the Bullion King Mine, which is not the same as this site. Don't get the sites mixed up, or better still, just go to both of them.

Rockhounding

The material here consists of limonite pseudomorphs after pyrite. They occur primarily as little cubes averaging about three-sixteenths of an inch on a side. A few range up to a half inch or so, and some occur as clusters. They are pyrite with a reddish brown coating of limonite and are found in a gray matrix. You won't have to hunt, since they are all over the place. The tailings to the left of the road as it crosses the creek are a good place to start, but the ridges to the northwest are just as good. The cliffs along the jeep road on the way up have many outcroppings that contain the cubes. They are usually fairly easy to remove from the matrix, but if you find an especially large one or a twin or cluster, take as much of the matrix as you need with you and work on removing the cube at home. If it is really nice and doesn't want to come out of the matrix, just leave it and trim the matrix to make a nice display.

View from Site 29.

Site 29

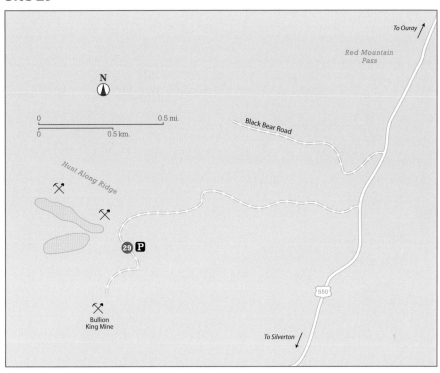

Road leading to Bullion King Mine.

30. US Basin

At 12,000 feet in US Basin.

Land type: High mountains.
Elevation: 12,000 feet.
GPS: N37 52.660' / W107 42.535'
Best season: Late spring through early fall.
Land manager: San Juan National Forest.
Material: Agate and jasper.
Tools: Rock hammer.
Vehicle: Four-wheel drive.
Accommodations: Motels, RV parking, and camping in Ouray and Silverton areas.
Special attractions: Many old mine dumps.
Finding the site: Head north on US 550 at Silverton toward Ouray for 5.6 miles to an unmarked jeep road to the right. US 550 twists and turns through here, so keep a sharp eye out for the turn. You won't confuse it, since there are no other roads nearby, but you do come upon it quickly. Follow the jeep road for 3.7 miles. You will cross the tailings pile of the Old Brooklyn Mine. If you have the time, you

might want to look around for mineral specimens. We haven't done that, but it looks like a fair possibility. Continue past the tailings for another 0.2 mile. Here you will see a caved-in mine on your left. Once again, this might be a good place to explore. Finally in another 1.5 miles, the road will turn to the right past a hillside and start down into United States Basin. At this point, you will be well above the 12,000-foot elevation mark. The GPS reading was taken next to the parking area. Pull off into the meadow and park. This road was opened and plowed when we were there in June 2015 as it is used as a back-road jeep trail. Remember to watch for vehicles traveling on this road as it is only a one lane and if you drop off the side it will be a while before you reach the bottom. One of the few places that I have been to where we were looking down on an elk herd and not up.

Rockhounding

Hunt on the hillsides to the east for jasper and banded agate. The agate occurs mostly as broken pieces of seam agate. Many seams are visible, however, and it is possible that a little digging and hard-rock mining will turn up some big, solid pieces.

Site 30

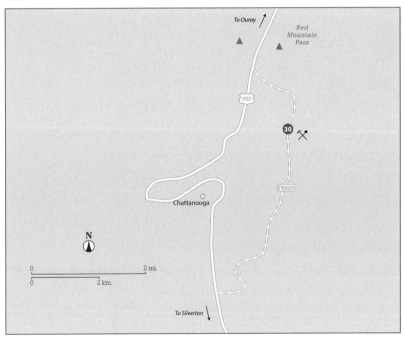

31. Silverton Mines

One of the many mines around Silverton.

Land type: Mountains.
Elevation: 9,318 feet at Silverton; mines range up to 12,000 feet.
Elevation at GPS site: 9,481 feet.
GPS: N37 49.452' / W107 30.115'
Best season: Summer.
Land manager: BLM, San Juan National Forest, and private.
Material: Mineral specimens.
Tools: Rock hammer and small digging tools.
Vehicle: Any to four-wheel drive.
Accommodations: Motels, hotels, and campground in Silverton.
Special attractions: San Juan Historical Society museum in Silverton and historic town of Silverton.

Finding the site: Any road out of Silverton will take you past mine dumps and tailings piles, but the best exploring will be done with four-wheel drive or serious hiking. As with many of the other big mining areas, it is a good idea to get some local information about what is open and what is closed to collecting. The GPS site was taken by the first tailings pile and the tailing sites go up the canyon from there.

Rockhounding

Keep your eyes open for samples of quartz (maybe even with a little gold, but don't hold your breath), galena, pyrite, sphalerite, chalcopyrite, rhodochrosite, rhodonite, calcite, and fluorite.

Site 31

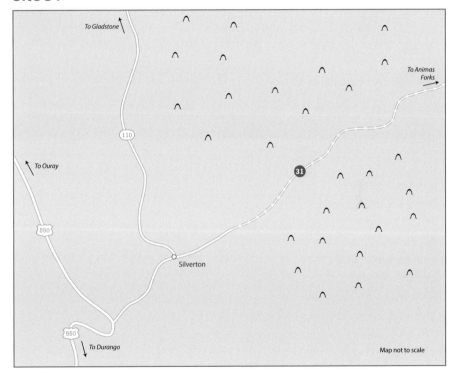

32. Aspen Mine

Keep to the lower road for Aspen Mine.

Land type: Mountains.
Elevation: 10,065 feet.
GPS: N37 49.213' / W107 37.657'
Best season: Late spring through early fall.
Land manager: BLM.
Material: Fluorite.
Tools: Rock hammer.
Vehicle: Four-wheel drive.
Accommodations: Motels, RV parking, and camping in Silverton area.
Special attractions: Many old mines and museum in Silverton.
Finding the site: This site is a little tricky to find. There are so many roads going everywhere in this area that it is very easy to take a wrong one. The good news is that there is usually something worthwhile to see or to collect along every one of them. We would also recommend that you forget your odometer readings

after you cross the Animas River. It is only a mile or so to the Aspen Mine, and trying to read tenths of a mile on an odometer while bouncing along in a jeep is not worth the effort. Not only are they hard to read, but odometers are very inaccurate on such terrain. Begin your trip at the north end of the main street in Silverton. Take CO 110 east toward Howardsville and Eureka. At just under 2 miles, you will see a tram line with a bucket hanging from it crossing overhead. To the right an unmarked road drops down and crosses the Animas River. This is the road up Arrastra Gulch. Follow it a short distance to the first of several forks. The main road goes uphill and this fork drops down to the creek. Turn right at the fork and drive across the bridge to the next fork. If you would like a short side trip to a great view from the top of the old Silver Lake Mill, take this fork to the right. After your explorations, continue on up the road to the Aspen Mine. The next fork has a big boulder with dead end, private property painted on it. Believe it. It ends at a private cabin. Continue past a couple of forks to the left. At about 0.1 mile past the second left-hand fork, you will pass the bottom of the tailings of the Aspen Mine and enter the ruins of the old town. Park and wander around this interesting old area. The GPS site was taken at this area.

Rockhounding

When you have had your fill of sightseeing, search the tailings at the mine for nice specimens of clear and pale green fluorite.

The Aspen is only one of many mines in this area. In fact, the Little Giant, located close by in Little Giant Basin, was the first of the early mines that unlocked the vast treasures of the San Juans. The Little Giant arrastra, from which the gulch gets its name, was a marvel of 1800s "high tech." The basic extraction method this tool employed was the same as for any other arrastra. The ore was pulverized by dragging rocks over it in a circle. The difference with this one was in the method of dragging the rocks. Where the original Spanish arrastra used mules walking in a circle to do the job, the Little Giant arrastra used a water wheel. This made for a device that ran constantly and only required someone to keep it filled with ore.

Explore this area. Visit the museum in Silverton. Absorb the history and collect some great mineral samples for your collection at the same time.

Old cabin by Aspen Mine.

Site 32

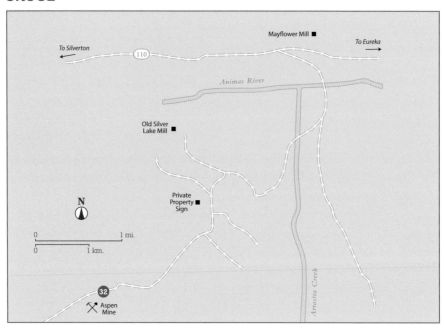

Slag pile and remains of sluice at Aspen Mine.

33. Eureka Gulch

Sunnyside Mill.

Land type: High mountains.
Elevation: 9,885 feet.
GPS: N37 52.854' / W107 33.988'
Best season: Late spring through early fall.
Land manager: BLM.
Material: Rhodonite.
Tools: Rock hammer.
Vehicle: Any to Eureka but high-clearance beyond.
Accommodations: Motels, RV parking, and camping in Silverton area.
Special attractions: Old mining area and museum in Silverton.
Finding the site: From the north end of Silverton, take CO 110 for approximately 7.5 miles to the old Eureka townsite. Although nothing remains of the town but a flat spot and a few old foundations, you will know when you are there by the huge

ruins of the Sunnyside Mill on the hillside to the north of the road. The road makes a 90-degree turn to the left, crosses the Animas River, and makes a 90-degree turn to the right just across the bridge. Park here to explore the area.

Rockhounding

Look over the area on the south side of CO 110 at the base of the hills for about a mile back toward Silverton. Railroad spurs used to run here, and you can find small piles of ore containing rhodonite along the old railbed.

If you have a high-clearance vehicle or four-wheel drive, take the road to the left, which crosses the top of the mill ruins and goes up to the old Sunnyside Mine and Lake Emma. Hunt for rhodonite along both sides of this road, but pay particular attention to the bottom of the drop-offs to the left as you ascend. A lot of ore trucks have made this run over the years, and a lot of ore fell off and ended up at the bottom of the hill. The rhodonite in this area is covered with a black "skin," which effectively disguises some of the prettiest pieces. Use your rock hammer to knock a little window on the end or side of a piece to see if the beautiful deep pink is hiding in there. Unfortunately, as with most such ventures, there is a lot of black material with innards that look as appealing as an old piece of sidewalk. Persevere, though, and you will be rewarded.

Caution: There are a number of old mines and tailings piles along this road, but many of them are on private property and closed. Be sure to respect the wishes of the property owners. Don't trespass. Make sure you have permission before collecting on any private property in this area.

If you continue up the road, you will come to the site of the original Sunnyside Mine. The site has been closed off and on for years, and we are not sure of its status now. We do know, however, that the reason for going up there has been removed. Once, the Sunnyside and its buildings huddled around Lake Emma, a glacial tarn at an altitude of 12,500 feet. Mining at this site ceased many years ago, but the lower mines had tunneled throughout the mountain. In fact, they ran tunnels from the main portal at Gladstone to the north of Silverton so far up into the mountain that in the summer of 1978 Lake Emma

Mines are abundant in this area.

broke through and dumped over a million tons of mud and water down the shafts. The force of the deluge flattened a twenty-ton locomotive in the mine and completely drained the lake through the Gladstone portal. Through a stroke of luck, the accident happened on a Sunday when no one was working in the mine. Consequently, there were no deaths or injuries. It was two years, though, before mining could resume.

A berm was bulldozed in the basin once occupied by Lake Emma to keep the snowmelt from running down the hole and through the mine. We went up there to see this place several years ago, and it was awesome. The old mine buildings and the tailings lining the "banks" of that former lake were a sight to behold. Unfortunately for all of us who love to travel and see these historic sites, the hole has now been filled in, the berms have all been smoothed out, the tailings have been hauled away, and the old buildings have been removed. It is still a beautiful spot, though, so bring your camera.

Site 33

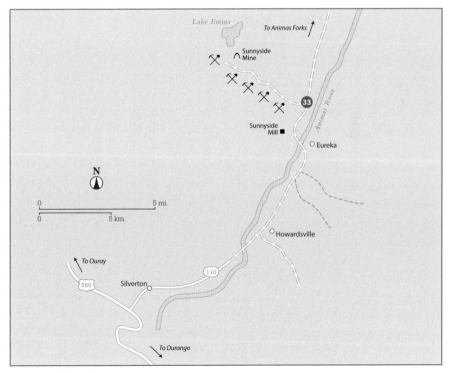

34. Placer Gulch

Coming into Placer Gulch.

Land type: High mountains.
Elevation: 11,154 feet.
GPS: N37 55.943' / W107 34.305'
Best season: Late spring through early fall.
Land manager: BLM.
Material: Rhodonite.
Tools: Rock hammer.
Vehicle: Four-wheel drive.
Accommodations: Motels, RV parking, and camping in Silverton area.
Special attractions: Old mining area, wildflowers in season, and museum in Silverton.
Finding the site: From the north end of Silverton, take CO 110 east a little more than 7 miles to the old Eureka townsite. Any vehicle will get you this far, but from here the next 7 miles to Animas Forks require a high-clearance vehicle. We

have seen lots of passenger cars on this road, but you would really have to hate your vehicle to do that to it. Animas Forks is an interesting old ghost town, and you should try to spend a little time there. It has a special attraction for us: The house that Cora's grandfather built around 1904 is still there, although a century of winters at 11,700 feet have taken their toll. We took the GPS at Animus Forks. When you have used up your film in Animas Forks, take the lower road (the one that runs right through the town) northwest across the little bridge over the Animas River for 0.6 mile. If you are an experienced mountain driver, you can make this trip with a high-clearance vehicle, but four-wheel drive is strongly recommended. At 0.6 mile, you will be at the lower end of the Bagley Mill. This beautiful old structure is also giving way to time and the elements. If you look around the inside—be careful in there—you will notice numbering on the old timbers. This huge mill was a kit. It was cut, fitted, numbered, and taken to the site for assembly. Continue up the road for another 0.5 mile to where the road forks. Take the left fork, cross the stream, and head out Placer Gulch toward the Gold Prince Mine. From the fork, it is a little less than 2 miles to the Gold Prince. On the way, you will see the restored Sound Democrat Mill on your left. It is a little rough getting over to it, but even if you have to hoof it, the effort won't be wasted. There is no collecting at the mill, but your camera will get a workout.

Rockhounding

Hunt all along the road and out onto the flats for rhodonite. The chunks you will find are almost all uniformly black, but not all contain rhodonite by any means. One clue is weight. The heavier pieces are more apt to contain what you are after. Unfortunately, not all of the heavy ones are rhodonite either. Prepare yourself to knock a lot of windows into a lot of rock if you plan to go home with some of the pretty pink stuff. The tailings

California Gulch sign by Placer Gulch.

at the foot of the old block wall at the Gold Prince were once a collecting spot, but this is private property and may be posted. Don't collect here without the owner's permission. If you are at this site in late summer or early fall and the snow is gone from the road, you can continue up behind the mine to the top of Treasure Mountain and down the other side. It is a spectacular trip on a four-wheel-drive.

Site 34

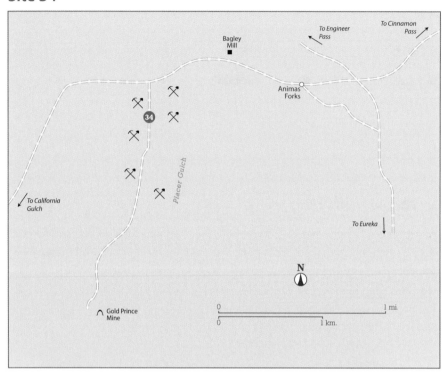

Building still stands in Placer Gulch and Animas Forks.

35. La Plata Canyon

La Plata Canyon slag pile.

Land type: High mountains.
Elevation: 11,600 feet at the top of Kennebec Pass.
Elevation at GPS site: 10,168 feet.
GPS: N37 25.931' / W108 02.330'
Best season: Spring through fall.
Land manager: San Juan National Forest.
Material: Picture stone and pyrite.
Tools: Rock hammer.
Vehicle: Any to campground, high-clearance to fork, and four-wheel drive to the top.
Accommodations: Motels, RV parking, and camping in Durango; and camping in La Plata Canyon.
Special attraction: La Plata Mining District.

Finding the site: From Durango go west on US 160 for about 11 miles. Take the well-marked La Plata County Road 124 north toward Mayday. The paved road winds over flatland for 4 miles to the old town of Mayday, where the pavement ends. A good dirt forest road continues for about 2 miles to the Kroeger Forest Service campground. This is a beautiful spot to camp while exploring the canyon.

Looking up La Plata Canyon.

The campground is in the trees, and the La Plata River is just across the road. If you are driving a passenger car, this is as far as you should go. Because of the snow at the top of the pass in June 2016, we were stopped at 11.5 miles before the road got too bad and snow packed. The GPS reading was taken at this area with a large tailings pile on the right. From here, you can find mines to explore and collect in. At Kennebec Pass, you can make all but the last 2 miles or so in a high-clearance vehicle. The last pitch to the pass is very steep and rocky. It is not dangerous in the sense that there are drop-offs and extremely narrow spots, but it does require four-wheel drive to pull it off. Continuing on from the campground, go a little more than 0.5 mile to the spot where the road crosses over Bedrock Creek. Just to the south of the creek, Bedrock Creek Road goes uphill to the left. If you have four-wheel drive, this is a nice side trip. The scenery is great, and the view from the Allard Mine at the top is spectacular. From the Bedrock Creek intersection, cross over the creek and walk up the hill, along the trail towards the Copper Hill Glory Hole, which is a gigantic hole that appears to be a caved-in mine. It is only 1.3 miles from the main road, but it feels like a hundred. Be aware that when you reach the mine, you will not be able to see it from the very large tailings pile and will have to scramble up the hill to the hole. The walls of the hole are covered with pyrite and the blue and green stains associated with copper minerals. You can collect nice samples of pyrite on the tailings, or you can chip them out of the walls. From Bedrock Creek, continue up the canyon to Kennebec Pass. There is a parking area there and Forest Service signs describing some hiking trails. At the parking area, you will have to make another decision. You will see a shelf road heading up to the east. This road goes to a spot called "The Notch." The Notch is where the nice picture stone is found, but the shelf road scares some people, and the turnaround at the top will probably have your passengers bailing out. Don't despair, however. We have driven the road, we have ridden as passengers, and we have walked it. If you want that picture stone badly enough, you can get there. **Caution:** If you decide to walk, the Notch is at almost 12,000 feet and the road to it is steep. If you are a flatlander, be sure you are up to the task before you try this hike. It is probably only a quarter mile or so, but it can feel like a lot more. This spot is also close to Parrot Peak and Root Gulch, the sites of two of Colorado's most famous lost mines. The Lone Wolf Mine is supposed to be somewhere near the base of Parrot Peak and is rumored to contain an extremely rich fissure vein of gold. The second is the Lost Clubfoot. This mine was discovered by a miner who was so secretive that he was known to hide his tools in the tunnel and throw the tailings in the stream so that no evidence of workings could be found. We guess it worked, since no one has reported finding it. On second thought, if you find a lost gold mine, would you report it?

Site 35

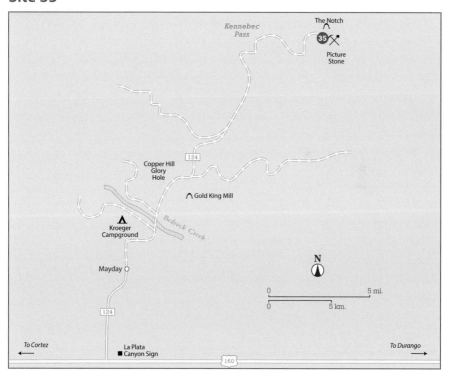

36. Rico Mines

Looking up the main street of Rico.

Land type: Mountains.
Elevation: 8,796 feet at Rico.
GPS: N37 41.673' / W108 01.907'
Best season: Summer.
Land manager: San Juan National Forest and private land.
Material: Mineral specimens.
Tools: Rock hammer, small digging tools, and screen.
Vehicle: Any to four-wheel drive.
Accommodations: Hotels, motels, and restaurants in Rico.
Special attraction: Mountain scenery.
Finding the site: Rico lies about midway between Dolores and Telluride on CO 145. Many mines can be seen from the highway, but be sure to take the side roads and trails, too. Because of the private property here, it will save you a lot of time and trouble if you make local inquiries before you head up those four-wheel-drive roads. Few things are more frustrating than fighting 10 miles of bad road only to come to a locked gate.

Rockhounding

We have passed through Rico numerous times on our way to and from other places, but have never done any hunting. It is a spot that should yield some nice mineral specimens if you can get to the mine dumps. There is a lot of private property around the area, and the town has become a summer retreat for many.

The first miners in the area were Spanish explorers who did some digging and built at least one smelting furnace. Prospectors arrived in the early 1800s, but the bad winters and trouble with the Indigenous people kept any serious work out of the area until the late 1870s when mining was legalized. Mines in the area worked fairly steadily through World War II, and tailings were reworked during the 1950s. The last mines closed in the early 1970s. During their working lives, the Rico mines produced silver, gold, copper, lead, and zinc. For the rockhound, there was sphalerite, galena, chalcopyrite, calcite, quartz, and rhodochrosite. Maybe there are even some samples left. In 2016, we stopped at the local city offices to inquire about rockhounding around Rico. They referred us to a mining office which was on Main Street and they told us that most of the area was under claim. Be sure to inquire before you go out to rock hunt in this area.

Site 36

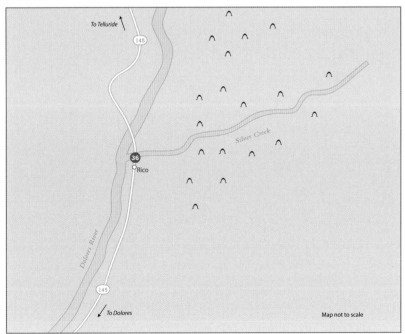

SOUTHEASTERN COLORADO

37. Meyers Ranch Roadcut

Parked by an outcrop of quartz and feldspar.

Land type: Highway roadcut.
Elevation: 8,977 feet.
GPS: N38 47.747' / W105 35.759'
Best season: Summer.
Land manager: Colorado State Highway Department.
Material: Quartz, pink feldspar, and muscovite mica.
Tools: Rock hammer.
Vehicle: Any.
Accommodations: Motels, RV parking, and campgrounds in Cañon City.
Special Attraction: Royal Gorge.
Finding the site: The roadcut is on the northeast side of CO 9, 6.5 miles north of the Guffey turnoff. If you are coming from the north, the site is 19.2 miles south of the junction of CO 9 and US 24 at Hartsel.

Rockhounding

Quartz, feldspar, and mica are abundant, even though this is a small pegmatite. Much of it is loose at the base of the cut, but it is easy to get material from the wall with a rock hammer. Please note that this is not a good place for small children. Although CO 9 is not heavily traveled, the site is very close to the road, and you will have to park in a small turnout about 0.2 miles south and walk back.

Quartz and pink feldspar are found in road-cuts in this area.

Site 37

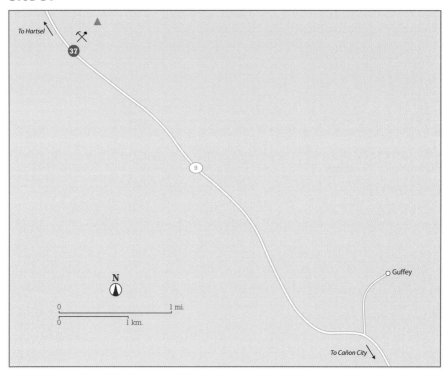

38. Garo

Check fields on both sides of the road for fluorescent agate.

Land type: Flat field.
Elevation: 9,186 feet.
GPS: N39 06.263′ / W105 53.436′
Best season: Summer.
Land manager: BLM.
Material: Fluorescent agate.
Tools: Rock hammer.
Vehicle: Any.
Accommodations: Motels, RV parking, and campgrounds in Buena Vista and Woodland Park.
Special attractions: None.
Finding the site: From the junction of US 24 and CO 9, at Hartsel, go north on CO 9 for 7.1 miles to the junction with Park County Road 24. At the junction, go southwest on CR 24 for about 0.3 mile and search the fields on both sides of the road for a mile or so. When we were there in June 2015, the west side of this road had been fenced, so make sure that you inquire before crossing the fence to hunt.

Rockhounding

The material here is neither overly plentiful nor exceptionally beautiful, but it does fluoresce nicely under ultraviolet light. If you are a night owl, this might be a great place to wander around on a moonless night with the black light. This area is the site of an old uranium mine, so if you fancy that kind of stuff, bring along the old Geiger counter.

Finally, blue agate used to be the prize here. We didn't find any, but then, we haven't found a lot of things that others did. If you come up with a chunk of blue, don't send us any letters to gloat.

Site 38

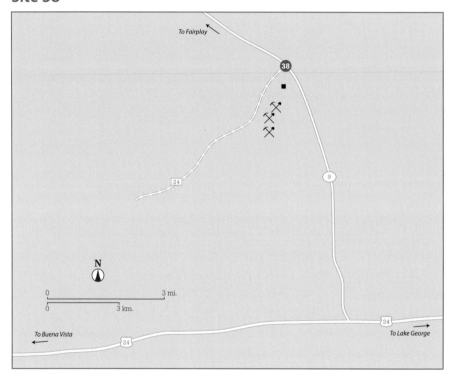

39. Wilkerson Pass

Mine on hillside at site on Wilkerson Pass.

Land type: Mountains.
Elevation: 9,403 feet.
GPS: N39 02.165' / W105 30.913'
Best season: Spring through fall.
Land manager: Pike National Forest.
Material: Muscovite, biotite, malachite, and azurite.
Tools: Rock hammer.
Vehicle: Any.
Accommodations: Motels, RV parking, and camping in Buena Vista and Fairplay areas; and RV parking and camping in Woodland Park.
Special attractions: None.
Finding the site: Wilkerson Pass is on US 24 between Lake George and Hartsel. From the visitor center at the pass, go east on US 24 for 0.5 mile. A dirt track leads to the north. The track is a little hard to see until you are right on it, so keep your eyes peeled. This is also a busy road, and stopping to turn can be a dangerous

proposition. Our plan was to go east, spot the road, continue to a turnaround spot, and go back to the track where we can make a safer right turn. The track gets a little rough, so just go as far as you feel comfortable, then park and walk to the mine, which is easily seen on the hillside. It is only a few hundred yards, and you can't drive right to the mine anyway.

Rockhounding

The tailings around the mine are full of nice samples of muscovite and biotite micas in a rainbow of colors. There are also good specimens of malachite and azurite for the display case. Nothing here is solid enough to cut and polish, but the mineral samples are nice, and the range of colors in the mica is spectacular. Galena and black tourmaline have been reported here, but we didn't have any luck finding either. For you boulder bashers, there are lots of nice schist outcroppings in the hills behind the mine.

Site 39

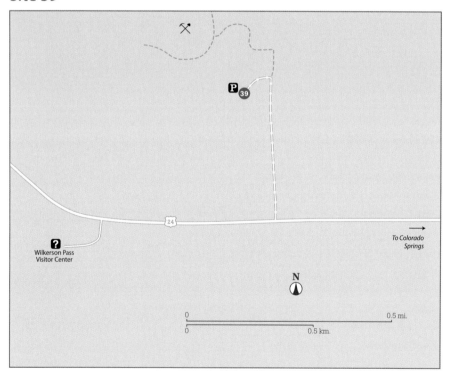

40. Lake George

Watch for this area to park.

Land type: Mountains.
Elevation: 7,973 feet.
GPS: N38 58.206' / W105 21.740'
Best season: Spring through fall.
Land manager: Pike National Forest.
Material: Feldspar, quartz, and mica.
Tools: Rock hammer, heavy hammer, and chisels.
Vehicle: Any.
Accommodations: Motels in Manitou Springs and Colorado Springs; and RV parking and camping in Lake George and Woodland Park areas.
Special attraction: Pikes Peak.
Finding the site: Lake George is on US 24 about midway between Colorado Springs and Buena Vista. From the center of Lake George, take Eleven Mile Canyon Road south 0.8 mile to an easily seen old mine on the left-hand side of the road. Park in the pullout on the side road.

Rockhounding

Closest to the road is a flooded pit. It may be tempting to climb down and inspect the walls of the pit, but it is unnecessary and can be hard to get back out. There is material in abundance on the surrounding hillsides. This site contains very nice pieces of both pink and orange feldspar, feldspar with quartz, and feldspar and quartz with mica books. On the hill behind the pit are good spots to attack with your chisel and heavy hammer. With a little care, nice specimens can be found here. Be careful in trying to remove the whole specimen on site. It is better to lug a little extra matrix home and cut it off with the proper tools than to break a really nice specimen.

Site 40

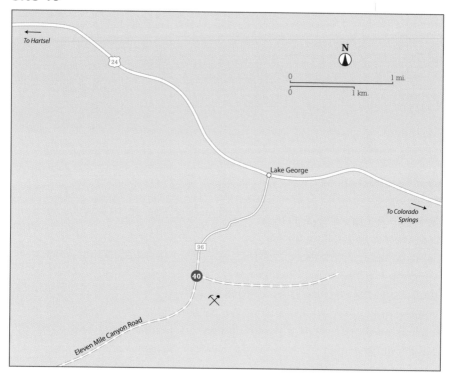

41. Round Mountain Campground

Nice pieces of quartz can be found here.

Land type: Mountains.
Elevation: 8,550 feet.
GPS: N39 01.870' / W105 25.058'
Best season: Spring through fall.
Land manager: Pike National Forest.
Material: Mica and quartz.
Tools: Rock hammer.
Vehicle: Any.
Accommodations: Motels in Manitou Springs and Colorado Springs; RV parking and camping (public and private) in Lake George and Woodland Park areas; and national forest campground at Round Mountain.
Special attraction: Pikes Peak.
Finding the site: Begin the trip in Lake George, which is on US 24 approximately 40 miles northwest of Colorado Springs. From Lake George, go 3.7 miles northwest on US 24 to a point where a road with a sign for a guest ranch goes

right. Don't let this stop you, just continue up the road. Take this road for 0.4 mile to where another unmarked road goes right. Turn onto this road and park. This is where the GPS was taken. Just ahead is a fence with a private property sign. Please observe this sign. Although I refer to this location as the Round Mountain Campground site, the actual campground is a bit farther west on US 24. If you reach the campground turnoff, you missed your road.

Rockhounding

Don't despair because the area behind the fence, which used to be open to collecting, is closed. There is a lot of nice material all over this area, and it is a beautiful spot to take a break. You did remember the camera and lunch?

Site 41

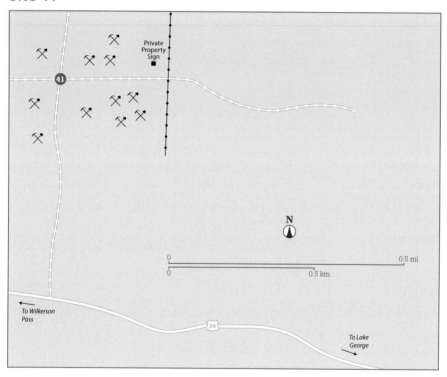

42. Highway 24 Roadcuts

Watch for roadcut that holds feldspar and mica.

Land type: Mountain highway.
Elevation: 8,445 feet.
GPS: N38 56.849' / W105 15.435'
Best season: Summer.
Land manager: Colorado State Highway Department.
Material: Pink feldspar with quartz and mica.
Tools: Rock hammer.
Vehicle: Any.
Accommodations: Motels, RV parking, and campgrounds in Lake George and Woodland Park areas.
Special attraction: Florissant Fossil Beds National Monument.
Finding the site: One of the best spots starts on US 24, 1.4 miles east of the junction with CR 1 in Florissant. The cliffs along the highway for miles are full of good material. The trick is in finding a good place to park. Keep an eye on the kids.

Rockhounding

The material is plentiful, and when the sun is right, the cliffs twinkle from the mica. Look for a place to pull off and park, and do a little walking.

Site 42

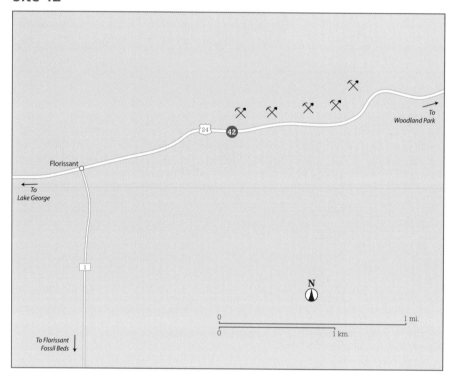

43. Florissant Fossil Beds National Monument

Petrified tree stumps.

Land type: Mountains.
Elevation: 8,377 feet.
GPS: N38 54.814' / W105 17.082'
Best season: Spring through fall.
Land manager: Florissant Fossil Beds National Monument.
Material: Fossil trees (no collecting).
Tools: None.
Vehicle: Any.
Accommodations: Motels in Manitou Springs and Colorado Springs; and RV parking and camping in Lake George and Woodland Park areas.
Special attraction: Florissant Fossil Beds National Monument.
Finding the site: From the town of Florissant, take Teller County Road 1 south for

2.3 miles to the turnoff to park headquarters. The visitor center at the headquarters has displays, books, and maps of various hiking trails.

Large petrified tree stump at Site 43.

About the site: The Florissant Fossil Beds contain some of the most beautiful and finely detailed plant and insect fossils in the world. Although they were known to exist by ranchers in the area in the early 1800s, it was much later that the true value of these fossils to science was recognized. In the early 1900s, serious scientific investigations began, and these continued for many years. It wasn't until 1969, however, that Congress declared nearly 6,000 acres of the site the Florissant Fossil Beds National Monument. Compared to the time it took for the beds to form, the time needed to declare it a national treasure was just the blink of an eye. The beds date back to the early Oligocene Epoch, about 35 million years ago. At that time, a series of volcanic eruptions in the volcanic field about 15 miles south of the monument covered the existing forest of giant sequoias with volcanic debris to a depth of about 15 feet. This allowed the tops of the trees to decay normally, while the stumps, trapped in the debris, were gradually subjected to the mineral replacement process. Still later in the Oligocene Epoch, mud flowing from the field blocked south-flowing streams and created Lake Florissant. Over a period of 100,000 years or more, intermittent eruptions dropped layers of volcanic ash over the lake area and created layer upon layer of sediment that trapped insects and plants in what would become shale. Finally, continuing flows of mud and ash formed a hard caprock that protected the fragile layers of fossil-filled shales. About 29 million years ago, the whole area from Kansas to Utah was uplifted 5,000 feet in a huge dome. The bottom of Lake Florissant, which had been at an altitude of about 3,000 feet, was now at more than 8,000 feet. The forces of wind and rain began their relentless attack on the caprock and finally exposed the fossil-bearing shales in many spots. Thanks to upheaval, erosion, and Congress, we are able to look back 35 million years and wonder at the flora and fauna that have been preserved in the Florissant shales. Remember to leave the rock hammer in the car since collecting is not allowed, but don't forget the camera.

Site 43

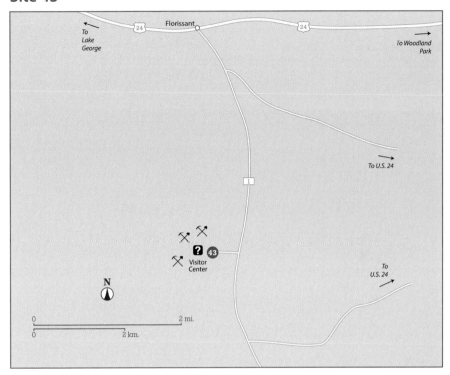

44. Florissant Fossil Quarry

Florissant Fossil Quarry.

Land type: Mountains.
Elevation: 8,213 feet.
GPS: N38 56.608' / W105 17.271'
Best season: Summer.
Land manager: Private.
Material: Plant and insect fossils.
Tools: Sharp knife or similar tool for splitting shale.
Vehicle: Any.
Accommodations: Motels, RV parking, and campgrounds in Lake George and Woodland Park areas.
Special attraction: Florissant Fossil Beds National Monument.
Finding the site: From US 24 at Florissant, go south on Teller County Road 1 for a quarter mile to the site on the right.

Rockhounding

If you have been to the Florissant Fossil Beds National Monument just down the road, you know about the incredibly detailed insect and plant fossils that abound in this area of Colorado. You know that the fossils are approximately 35 million years old, and you know that you can't collect them. If this latter fact has you frustrated, then this is the site for you. The quarry, which is on private land, has been in the Clare family for more than fifty years. The fossils are in the same formation as those at the national monument, but it is perfectly legal to collect these, and people from all walks of life do just that every summer. In fact, you may find yourself rubbing elbows with students and scientists who have come to study, or with folks who just discovered the world of fossils and collecting and want to give it a try. For a nominal fee, you can join them and collect some of the beautiful material and have fun doing it. The friendly folks at the quarry will show you how to split the shale and help you identify what you find.

To find out more, you can reach the folks at the site by phoning (719) 748-1002 or (719) 748-3275 or sending an e-mail to florissantfossils@yahoo .com. To see photos of fossils found at the quarry, visit their website at www .members.tripod.com/florissantfossils.

Site 44

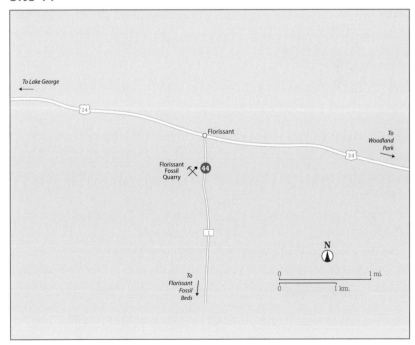

45. Opportunity Mine

Site of Opportunity Mine.

Land type: Mountains.
Elevation: 8,361 feet.
GPS: N38 31'02.16" / W106 40'04.14"
Best season: Spring through fall.
Land manager: BLM.
Material: Feldspar, beryl, mica, cleavelandite, and black tourmaline.
Tools: Rock hammer.
Vehicle: Any.
Accommodations: Motels, RV parking, and camping in Gunnison area.
Special attraction: Curecanti National Recreation Area.
Finding the site: From Parlin, which is about 12 miles east of Gunnison on US 50, take Gunnison County Road 76 for 3.8 miles to CR 44, road on the right. Follow this road for 0.7 mile and park off the road. You will see the old Opportunity Mine on the hillside to your right. There is a jeep road to the mine, but when we were there,

it was blocked with boulders. It is a short walk, though, and you can collect material all the way to the mine.

Feldspar, mica outcropping at Opportunity Mine.

Rockhounding

There is a lot of feldspar and mica here, which is very showy, but the best we found was blue beryl in a white variety of albite called cleavelandite. We were told that this is somewhat rare, but in any case it is pretty. We also found a bit of black tourmaline, which looks very nice against the white matrix. Although we didn't find any, there are pink lepidolite flakes reported in this area. Maybe you will be lucky.

Site 45

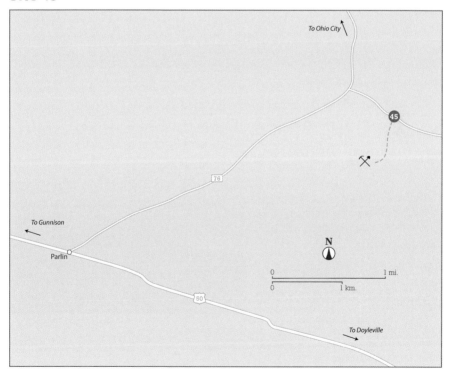

46. Cochetopa Dome

This cut holds lots of Apache tears.

Land type: Roadcut.
Elevation: 8,991 feet.
GPS: N38 13.861' / W106 44.816'
Best season: Spring through fall.
Land manager: Saguache County Highway Department.
Material: Apache tears.
Tools: Rock hammer.
Vehicle: Any.
Accommodations: Motels, RV parking, and camping in Gunnison area.
Special attractions: None.

Cochetopa Dome.

Finding the site: To reach the Cochetopa Dome site, drive east from Gunnison on US 50 to the intersection of CO 114. Go south on CO 114 for 20.2 miles to Saguache County Road NN14. Turn right onto CR NN14 and proceed for 4.1 miles to the intersection of CR KK14. Continue just past the intersection and park along the large roadcut on the left side of CR NN14. If coming from Saguache, don't take the first CR NN14 turnoff. There is another one just down the road from this.

Rockhounding

Hunt along the roadcut, which extends for a few hundred yards. This cut has lots and lots of Apache tears just for the picking. We were there on a rainy day and had to wait for a break in the rain, jump out of the car, hop over the water-filled ditch, and run up the hill to grab a few tears before the next shower. Even with these less-than-desirable conditions, we found a nice pile of the little obsidian treasures. Although some of them are big enough to cut into cabochons, most Apache tears are best left to the tumbler.

Site 46

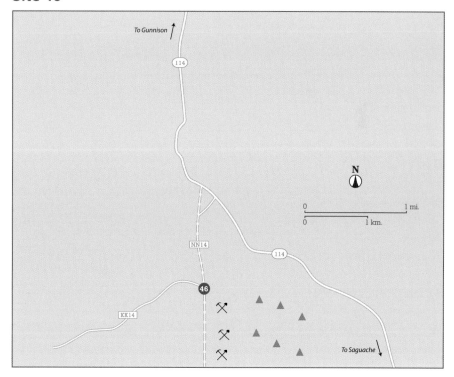

47. Crystal Hill

This area is fenced off, and a sign will tell you of any mining in the area.

Land type: Mountains.
Elevation: 8,969 feet.
GPS: N37 50'30.05" / W106 16'57.01"
Best season: Spring through fall.
Land manager: BLM.
Material: Amethyst and quartz crystals.
Tools: Rock hammer and digging tools.
Vehicle: Any.
Accommodations: Motels, RV parking, and camping in Del Norte and Monte Vista areas.
Special attraction: Museum at Saguache.
Finding the site: To reach the Crystal Hill Mine, begin your trip at the intersection of US 285 and CO 114 in Saguache. Drive south on US 285 for 17.4 miles. Take Saguache County Road 41G west for 4.8 miles. The road makes a 90-degree turn to the north and crosses CR 41G at La Garita. Go straight at the intersection. This

is CR 42. Follow it for 2.2 miles to the intersection of CR 42K. Turn left and follow CR 42K for about 6 miles. You will see the roads cut into the hillside at the Crystal Hill Mine. You cannot see the main pit from the road. Drive along the foot of the tailings until you see a road going up the hill to your right. There will be a locked gate a few yards up the road. Park along here and hike up the road past the gate. A short way up the hill, another old mine roadcuts back to your left. Follow this to the main pit. It is partially blocked just before the pit, but don't turn back as we did. Just beyond the boulders blocking the road is the main pit floor. It is quite a sight. This was a large open-pit operation in the 1970s and looks like a miniature of the Bingham Canyon Copper Mine in Utah.

Rockhounding

The Crystal Hill Mine was closed to collecting for years after mining operations ceased. This was evidently due to the cyanide used in the leaching operations. We poked around the rusty looking boulders along the road and found some nice crystal formations, but they were not museum quality by any means. While we were still looking, it began to rain, so

Road leading to mine.

we headed for the La Garita store just west of the intersection of CR G, CR 38, and CR 42. The owner of the store said the mine was no longer closed to collecting.

A BLM employee confirmed that collecting is allowed and that the floor of the pit is a good place to start. The real prizes here are amethyst crystals. Needless to say, we found none. It is our understanding that some serious hard-rock mining in the walls of the pit are necessary to break open crystal-bearing cavities. You have our blessing. We wandered around the floor of the pit and found a nice little collection of clear quartz crystals. It is not even necessary to dig for them. Just get the sun in the right place, and they twinkle at you.

Caution: The ground here has a very high content of black manganese oxide, so it is best to wear old clothes. If you just pick up the surface crystals, however, you will not get dirty. Dig just a little, and it is a different story.

Site 47

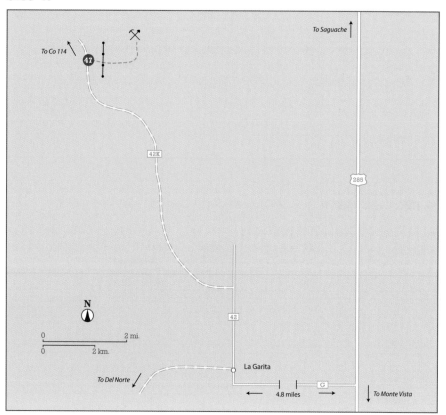

To Co 114

To Saguache

42K

285

N

0   2 mi.
0   2 km.

42

La Garita

To Del Norte

4.8 miles

G

To Monte Vista

48. Houselog Creek

Road into Houselog Creek.

Land type: Mountains.
Elevation: 9,276 feet.
GPS: N38 03.010′ / W106 23.786′
Best season: Spring through fall.
Land manager: Rio Grande National Forest.
Material: Geodes.
Tools: Rock hammer and digging tools.
Vehicle: Any.
Accommodations: Motels, RV parking, and camping in Del Norte and Monte Vista areas; and RV parking and camping in Saguache area.
Special attraction: Museum in Saguache.
Finding the site: From Saguache follow CO 114 west for 14.8 miles to the intersection of Saguache County Road 41G. Turn south onto CR 41G and proceed

6.4 miles to a well-marked Forest Service road leading to Lower South Park. Park on the flat at the intersection and hunt on the hillside to the northwest.

This is a mine tailings area—check it out.

Rockhounding

You will find broken pieces of geodes all over the hillside. Most are filled with either jasper or banded agate. The loose pieces are small, and not all are worth taking home. This is a fair-sized area, though, and a little serious digging should still produce some excellent specimens. Even if you don't want to dig, there is plenty of material to pick over, and much of it will look nice in the display case.

Site 48

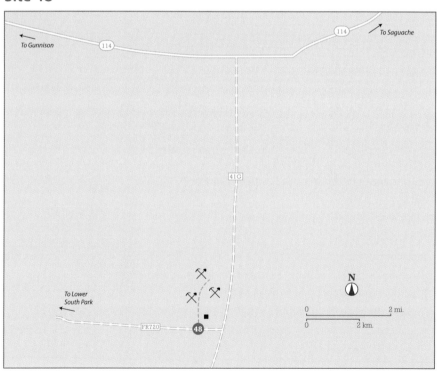

49. Creede

One of the many buildings still standing in Creede Canyon.

Land type: Mountains.
Elevation: 8,852 feet.
GPS: N37 49.771' / W106 55.081'
Best season: Spring through fall.
Land manager: Colorado Department of Transportation and Rio Grande National Forest.
Material: Fossils.
Tools: Rock hammer and small digging tools.
Vehicle: Any.
Accommodations: Motels, RV parking, and camping in Creede area.
Special attraction: Creede Mining District.
Finding the site: From South Fork, 15 miles west of Del Norte on US 160, go north on CO 149 for 21.5 miles to Creede. Continue through town and head west on CO 149 toward Lake City. About 1 mile from Creede, you will see a roadcut on the right. The road turns to the right at the end of the cut. There is a wide area for

parking here. Park and hunt on the hillside at the end of the cut, all along the cut, and up the little gullies.

Rockhounding

The Creede area is noted for the beautiful amethyst from its many old mines, and most guidebooks dwell on this. The fact is that the area is nearly all private, fenced, and posted. A few of the old tailings piles run down to the road and can be hunted, but virtually every rockhound in the northern hemisphere has already been there. The streams are a possibility, but we wouldn't recommend that you make the trip just to try for amethyst there. In fact, we talked to two old-timers who live nearby, and they said that the only amethyst they had ever found was in one fellow's driveway. It seems that the county highway department crushes tailings and uses the material for gravel. Maybe we should have asked directions to his driveway.

Don't be discouraged, though. The sights around Creede are unmatched. Visit the museums in town and be sure to go out of town to the north and look at the old mines hanging precariously to the sides of the cliffs. This is a unique mining area and one you and your camera shouldn't miss.

You will have better luck at the fossil area. This was an Oligocene Epoch lake bed that formed in much the same way as Lake Florissant. Fossils of both plants and insects can be found here. The roadcut exposes part of the old lake bed. The fossils at this site are small, and will take some hunting if you are to find nice ones, but they are there. Take a picnic lunch and plan to spend some time here.

Parked at Site 49—GPS taken here.

Sites 49-50

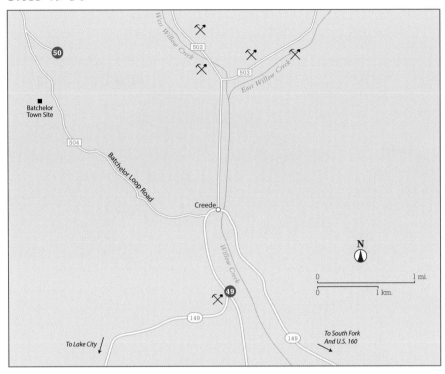

Old tailing dam north of Creede.

50. Last Chance Mine

Last Chance Mine.

See map on page 135.
Land Type: Mountains.
Elevation: 10,270 feet.
GPS: N37 53.047' / W106 56.233'
Best Season: Spring through fall.
Land Manager: Private claim with visitor rights.
Material: Copper, red jasper, galena, zinc, pink rhodonite, native silver, and sowbelly agate.
Tools: Rock hammer and bucket. Tools are also supplied at the mine.
Vehicle: Any vehicle up to the mine.
Accommodations: Motels and RV parking in Creede. Cabins are available for up to 12 people at the mine site for a donation amount.
Special attractions: None.
Finding the site: From the town of Creede, turn on Bachelor Road across from the Creede ball field and stay on the main road. When you reach the townsite of

Bachelor on your left, you will see the 4-mile marker, a small green sign on your right. Continue over the mountain for 1 mile; you will see the 5-mile marker. Turn right onto the Last Chance Mine Road. Stay on road for 0.5 mile and enter Last Chance Mine.

Old mining area at Last Chance Mine.

Rockhounding

This mine dates back 115 years. It is a private mine but welcomes visitors to the mine for tours and rockhounding. For information on this mine, go to http://lastchancemine.com. This is one you won't want to miss as you can pick up some very nice sowbelly agate, which is seam agate with amethyst running through the seam. This makes beautiful cabs and jewelry. On the website, you will see tours, a photo gallery, and other interesting information about this mine, including when it is accessible.

Cabin to stay in at mine.

51. Twin Mountains

Twin Mountains at Del Norte.

Land type: Mountains.

Elevation: 8,537 feet.

GPS: N37 45.785' / W106 25.880'

Best season: Spring through fall.

Land manager: Rio Grande National Forest.

Material: Agate.

Tools: Rock hammer.

Vehicle: Any to Old Woman Creek and four-wheel drive to upper site.

Accommodations: Motels, RV parking, and camping in Del Norte and Monte Vista.

Special attractions: None.

Finding the site: From the intersection of US 160 and CO 112 in Del Norte, go east on CO 112 for 0.5 mile. Turn north onto Rio Grande CR 22 and go 0.8 mile toward the airport. Go left on CR 15 for 2.8 miles to where the road forks. Take the right fork (FR 660) for 2.7 miles to a dirt road heading off to the left. At 1.1 miles, a fork goes right to a residence. Don't take the right fork. Keep straight for another 0.5 mile. Here the road forks around a house. Take the very rough left fork up the hill for another 0.5 mile where you will meet an unmarked Forest Service road. Turn left (south) and go 0.1 mile to where a dirt track goes up a little hill to the left. Drive or walk up this hill to the site of some old agate diggings. Retrace your route to the intersection of FR 66 and continue north for about 1 mile to where FR 646 forks to the left. This road is now G-32 and FR 66 turns into A-32 at the intersection where GPS was taken. Park along G-32 and hunt along Old Woman Creek to the north of the road.

Rockhounding

This is a vast collecting area, and the sites listed are only a small number of those that exist here. The Twin Mountains area has been collected by both rockhounds and commercial enterprises for many years. To get the best of what is here, you should spend several days. If you have a four-wheel drive, take any of the roads leading up into the Twin Mountains. There are many old commercial sites that still contain some fine cutting material.

GPS reading was taken at the forks of G–32 and A–32.

Don't overlook the flats around the base of the mountains and near the fork of G–32 and A–32. Two more sites in this area are a geode/septarian nodule site at GPS N37 45.457' / W106 27.333' El 8782, and a petrified wood site at GPS N37 45.253' / W106 26.258' El 8442.

Just park and look around for some nice agate.

Site 51

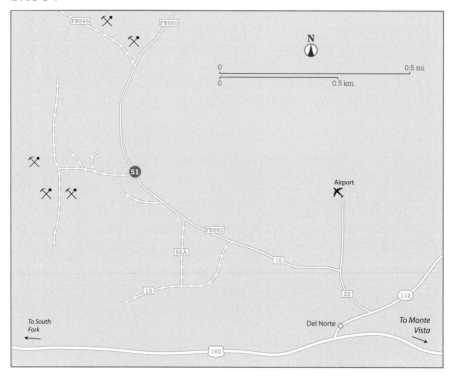

Septarian site.

52. Ruby Mountain

Ruby Mountain.

Land type: Mountains.
Elevation: 7,641 feet.
GPS: N38 45.147' / W106 04.211'
Best season: Spring through fall.
Land manager: BLM.
Material: Apache tears, garnet, and topaz.
Tools: Rock hammer, heavy hammer, and chisels.
Vehicle: Any.
Accommodations: Motels, RV parking, and camping in Buena Vista area; and camping at Arkansas River Recreation Area.
Special attraction: Arkansas River Recreation Area.
Finding the site: From the post office in Nathrop on US 285, drive 1.8 miles north to the intersection of Chaffee County Road 301. Turn right onto CR 301, cross the bridge, and continue 0.5 mile to CR 300. Go south on CR 300 about 2.5 miles to the recreation area. Take the left fork to the parking area at the foot of Ruby Mountain.

This is in the Arkansas River Recreation Area, and requires a day pass. The GPS was taken in the parking area in the recreation area.

Rockhounding

The real prizes at Ruby Mountain are garnet and yellow topaz. It will take some work and some luck to find them, but they are there. Most seem to be found at or near the top of the mountain, but be sure to keep your eyes open all along the trail to the top. Serious rockhounds use hammers and chisels to open up the rhyolite and expose crystal-containing cavities. There are also lots of easily found little Apache tears for you to shed in case you don't find the garnet and topaz.

Site 52

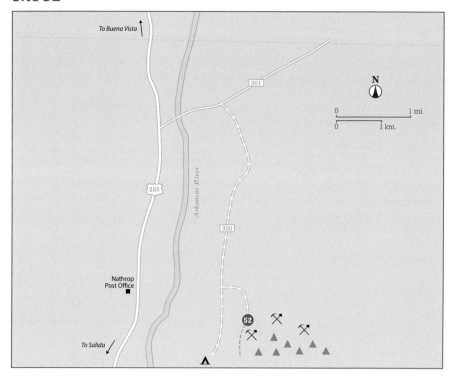

53. Mount Antero

Mount Antero.

Land type: High mountain.
Elevation: 14,269 feet.
Elevation at GPS site: 9,443 feet.
GPS: N38 42.601' / W106 17.499'
Best season: Summer.
Land manager: San Isabel National Forest.
Material: Aquamarine, beryl, topaz, garnet, and tourmaline.
Tools: Rock hammer, chisels, bars, and heavy hammer.
Vehicle: Four-wheel drive.
Accommodations: Motels, RV parking, and camping in Buena Vista area.
Special attractions: Many old mines.
Finding the site: The site may be Colorado's most famous gem-collecting area, and it is the highest gem collecting area in North America. From all accounts, the site is also one of the toughest to get to. If you decide to give it a try, your best source of information is a rock shop found at Mile Marker 138 on CO 285. They can

tell you the conditions of the road and mountain at the time you are going to Mount Antero. The rock shop is located between Buena Vista and Poncha Springs on US 285. Getting to the site: From Buena Vista, travel 8 miles to CR 162 on your right. Follow CO 162 for approximately 12 miles. Turn south onto FR 277. This road is marked by a sign about the Mount

Rough road going to Mount Antero.

Antero area. GPS reading was taken at this point. The road entrance is just across and to the west of CR 292 which goes to Alpine Lake. This is where the four-wheel drive fun begins. A sign warns of the extremely rough and dangerous road ahead. In talking with the rock shop owner, he said that from this sign to the parking area is anywhere from 3 to 4 hours of rough roads. The people that have claims in this area do take heavy equipment over this road and it takes them anywhere from 3 to 5 days to put their equipment into a site.

Rockhounding

The number and quality of the materials that have been found here are intriguing. The real prize is aquamarine, but smoky quartz, fluorite, topaz, phenakite, and beryl have also been found. The crystals are found in pockets in the granite and require some hard work with the hammer and chisel to free them. Of course, it is first necessary to find something to hammer on, so a lot of luck helps.

There are also a couple of practical matters to consider. Hard-rock mining at more than 14,000 feet is not for the faint (or weak) of heart. Serious consideration must be taken as to your overall physical condition before trying this trip. Remember also that the weather can change very rapidly at this altitude, so have warm clothing and foul-weather gear with you. Summer afternoon and evening thunderstorms are common. Lightning is not your friend up there. If it starts, the best policy is to leave.

If you are still determined to go, good luck. You may well go home with a real prize gem. Come to think of it, maybe we will see you up there.

Site 53

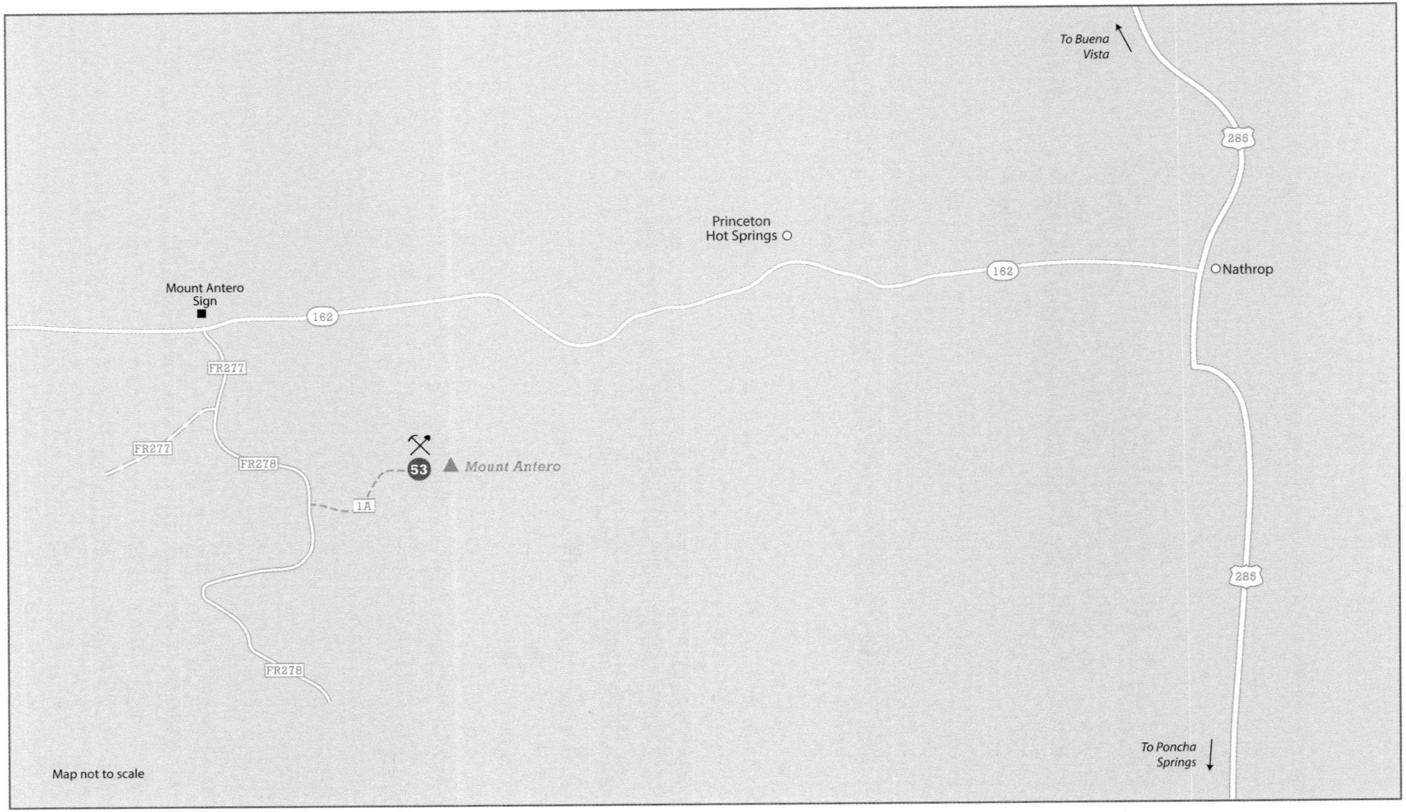

To Buena
Vista

285

Nathrop

To Poncha
Springs

285

162

Princeton
Hot Springs

162

Mount Antero

Mount Antero
Sign

1A

53

FR277

FR278

FR277

FR278

Map not to scale

54. Clara May Mine

Camping area for Clara May Mine (Site 54) and Midway Spring (Site 55).

Land type: Mountains.
Elevation: 8,890 feet.
GPS: N38 50.868' / W105 59.001'
Best season: Spring through fall.
Land manager: BLM.
Material: Rose quartz, smoky quartz, pink feldspar, and jasper.
Tools: Rock hammer.
Vehicle: Any.
Accommodations: Motels, RV parking, and camping in Buena Vista area.
Special attractions: None.
Finding the site: About 25 miles north of Poncha Springs, head east on US 24/285 for 6 miles to Chaffee CR 307. Turn right onto CR 307 and proceed for just less than 2 miles. Park in the little meadow on your right and hike up the old mine road to the left of the trees. The old road is a little hard to see, so keep a sharp eye out. If you come to CR 308, you just missed the old road. Turn around and go back

about 0.1 mile and you will see it on your left. It is only about a quarter-mile hike to the mine, and you will find material all along the way.

Rockhounding

The Clara May is an old mine with a small pit and a lot of tailings to explore. You will find very nice samples of rose quartz, smoky quartz, white quartz, and pink feldspar. The lure of this old site for us has been the possibility of finding some really nice jasper. In the 1972 edition of his book *Colorado Gem Trails*, Richard Pearl talks about his wife finding boulders of jasper on the hills behind the mine. We have looked a little bit and have found some very pretty chips and some small pieces, but we haven't found the source. Maybe we were at the wrong mine or the wrong hill, but we bet it is there somewhere. If you find the jasper source, leave some for us.

Site 54

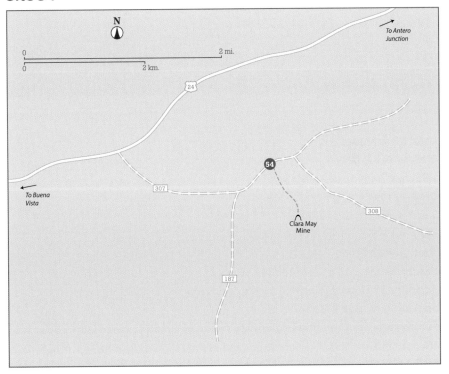

55. Midway Spring

Aragonite in the mine area.

Land type: Mountains.
Elevation: 8,815 feet.
GPS: N38 36.042' / W105 56.504'
Best season: Spring through fall.
Land manager: San Isabel National Forest.
Material: Aragonite and clear quartz.
Tools: Rock hammer.
Vehicle: Any.
Accommodations: Motels, RV parking, and camping in the Salida area.
Special attractions: Many old mines.
Finding the site: Start at the intersection of CO 291 and Chaffee County Road 153 just north of Salida. Go northeast across the Arkansas River bridge on CR 153 for 0.2 mile. Make a 90-degree turn to the right onto CR 175 (Spiral Drive). Follow CR 175 for 6.4 miles. CR 181 forks to the right. Park at the fork and climb the hill on the north side of CR 175 directly across from the fork. It may be a little hard to

scramble up the roadcut, so just walk along until you find an easy spot, climb to the top of the cut, and walk back. The site is about 15 or 20 yards up the hill in the trees. You won't be able to see it from the road, but once you are on top of the roadcut, you can follow the float, the scattered pieces of aragonite, right to it.

Rockhounding

The prime material here is a brown and white–banded aragonite, which looks very much like onyx. This whole hill has aragonite deposits, so take some time and find the best pieces. At the main site, there is a seam of calcite in a fan-shaped deposit about 3 or 4 feet thick. It is one of the prettiest seams of its kind that we have ever seen.

Sites 55-60

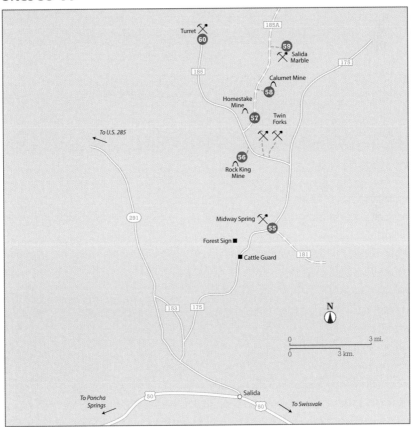

56. Rock King Mine

Tailings at Rock King Mine.

See map on page 149.
Land type: Mountains.
Elevation: 8,748 feet.
GPS: N38 37.414' / W105 57.480'
Best season: Spring through fall.
Land manager: San Isabel National Forest.
Material: Quartz, graphic granite, and radiating actinolite crystals.
Tools: Rock hammer.
Vehicle: Any.
Accommodations: Motels, RV parking, and camping in the Salida area.
Special attractions: Many old mines.
Finding the site: From Midway Spring (Site 55), proceed along CR 185 another 2.1 miles to where the road forks. Just before the fork you will see a track going off to the left. Follow this track past some old buildings until you drive onto the top of

the Rock King tailings. Park and hunt on and around the tailings.

Rockhounding

There are literally tons and tons of tailings to hunt on and around at this site. We found lots of quartz, some graphic granite, and very nice radiating actinolite crystals. The tailings are steep in places, so keep an eye on the kids.

Gary at Rock King Mine.

Rock King Mine tailings.

57. Homestake Mine

Homestake Mine Road.

See map on page 149.
Land type: Mountains.
Elevation: 8,816 feet.
GPS: N38 37.632' / W105 57.321'
Best season: Spring through fall.
Land manager: San Isabel National Forest.
Material: Feldspar, quartz, radiating actinolite crystals, and mica.
Tools: Rock hammer.
Vehicle: Any.
Accommodations: Motels, RV parking, and camping in the Salida area.
Special attractions: Many old mines.
Finding the site: From the Rock King Mine (Site 56), go onto the fork (Chaffee County Road 185). Take the right fork (Chaffee County Road 185A). In about 0.3 mile, you will see a pile of huge boulders on your left. Park and hunt on and around the boulders. On the other side of the boulder pile is a flooded quarry, so

be careful. It would be difficult to get out of the quarry if you should fall in. Be sure, also, to keep a sharp eye on the children.

Rockhounding

This is a very interesting site. Huge boulders are piled about 20 or so feet high just off the road on the side of the flooded quarry. Most of these boulders are literally covered

Another view of Homestake Mine.

with very nice examples of radiating, greenish actinolite crystals. Many have traces of reddish garnet in the matrix. It is easy to break samples off the boulders, but there are loose samples all over the ground at the foot of the boulder pile, too. Be selective and you will go home with some beautiful specimens.

A large boulder with quartz and mica at Homestake Mine.

58. Calumet Mine

Calumet Mine.

See map on page 149.
Land type: Mountains.
Elevation: 9,052 feet.
GPS: N38 38.404' / W105 57.255'
Best season: Spring through fall.
Land manager: San Isabel National Forest and private claim.
Material: Green epidote.
Tools: Rock hammer.
Vehicle: High-clearance.
Accommodations: Motels, RV parking, and camping in the Salida area.
Special attractions: Many old mines.
Finding the site: From the Homestake Mine (Site 57), continue up CR 185A. At just more than 0.5 mile, you will see some old concrete ruins near the creek on the left. Park along the side of the road and climb the steep trail that goes up the mountain to the right. This will take you to the old Calumet Iron Mine. The mine

cannot be seen from the road. This area now requires permission from the private owners to hunt on.

Rockhounding

Make inquiries in Salida before you try the trip. If it is open, you will stand a good chance of finding some of the relatives of the many gemstones that have come from this place. Currently, the prize is green epidote, but garnet, sapphire, and blue corundum have also been found.

59. Salida Marble

Salida Marble.

See map on page 149.
Land type: Mountains.
Elevation: 9,591 feet.
GPS: N38 39.389' / W105 57.758'
Best season: Spring through fall.
Land manager: San Isabel National Forest.
Material: White marble.
Tools: Rock hammer.
Vehicle: High-clearance and four-wheel drive.
Accommodations: Motels, RV parking, and camping in the Salida area.
Special attractions: Many old mines.
Finding the site: From the Calumet Mine (Site 58) parking area, continue along CR 185A for another 1.3 miles. You will see large workings on the hillside to the right. Follow the dirt track to the foot of the mine tailings.

Rockhounding

All over this area, in the tailings piles and on the quarry walls, you will find very nice, but somewhat coarse-grained, white marble. Many of the blocks have cavities with nice clear quartz crystals in them. Take some time and pick the best pieces.

60. Turret

A building in the old town of Turret.

See map on page 149.
Land type: Mountains.
Elevation: 8,517 feet.
GPS: N38 38.371' / W105 59.408'
Best season: Spring through fall.
Land manager: San Isabel National Forest.
Material: Pegmatite materials.
Tools: Rock hammer and chisels.
Vehicle: High-clearance.
Accommodations: Motels, RV parking, and camping in the Salida area.
Special attractions: Many old mines and ghost town.
Finding the site: From the fork at the Rock King Mine (Site 56), take the left fork, which is Chaffee CR 185, for about 2 miles to the remains of the town of Turret. Look for tailings on the hillsides and investigate them. There are many old mines and prospect holes in this area.

Rockhounding

Turret is now a town with new structures and homes. Most of the town is private, so we were not able to find anything worth digging for, but there is a lot of the old town still standing, which is interesting to see. Most of the old structures are on private and posted land, but there are many pegmatite outcroppings in the area. We didn't find anything to write home about, but there is a lot to explore, and beryl specimens have been reported here. So if you have some time to spend, chances are you will find some nice material for display.

61. Browns Canyon

Old mill ruins in Browns Canyon.

Land type: Mountains.
Elevation: 7,687 feet.
GPS: N38 39.182' / W106 03.904'
Best season: Spring through fall.
Land manager: BLM.
Material: Biotite mica and fluorspar.
Tools: Rock hammer.
Vehicle: Any or four-wheel drive.
Accommodations: Motels, RV parking, and camping in the Salida area.
Special attractions: None.
Finding the site: From the intersection of US 285 and CO 291 north of Poncha Springs, take US 285 north for about 1.5 miles to Chaffee County Road 194 (Hecla Junction). Go east on CR 194 for 1.6 miles. You will see an old mine off to your right. Where we took the GPS reading is on an improved road and the mine

sits to the right-hand side of the road. This area is now a national monument area, but there are no signs as yet telling you where the monument starts. Check with local authorities for references to this area.

Rockhounding

This is an old fluorspar mine, but we didn't find any fluorspar. Maybe we just wandered over good specimens. We have been known to do that. We did find nice pieces of feldspar with biotite mica, though. This was a fairly large operation, and there are lots of old foundations and tailings to explore. As usual, time and patience will probably pay off in some nice finds.

Site 61

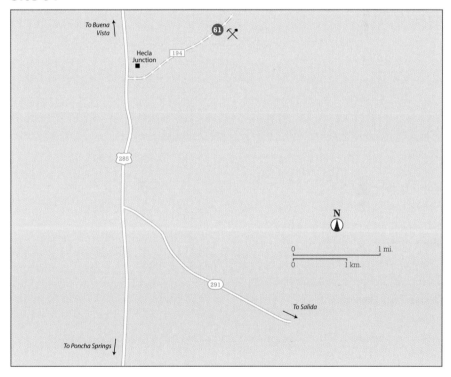

62. Marshall Pass

Old railroad bed at the top of Marshall Pass.

Land type: Mountains.
Elevation: 10,849 feet.
GPS: N38 23.693' / W106 14.858'
Best season: Spring through fall.
Land manager: San Isabel and Gunnison National Forests.
Material: Agate, jasper, and feldspar.
Tools: Rock hammer.
Vehicle: Any.
Accommodations: Motels, RV parking, and camping in the Salida area; and camping at O'Haver Lake.
Special attraction: Mountain railway pass.
Finding the site: Just northwest of Poncha Springs, go south on US 285 for 5.1 miles. Turn west onto FR 243 and follow the signs to Marshall Pass. There are several forks and FR 243 becomes FR 200, but the main road is easy to follow and well marked to Marshall Pass. The top of the pass is 13.5 miles west of the intersection at US 285. This

is a beautiful drive any time of year; but in the fall, when the aspens are turning, it is spectacular.

At the top of the pass, you will see the remains of an old loading ramp just to the right of the road. There is a wide parking area to the left of the road. Park here and roam all over, above the loading ramp and along the old railbed. Search the hillsides and the gullies for jasper and agate. There are places where the Forest Service has pushed berms up to block some of the old road, and these berms are good spots to hunt.

Park and walk through meadow for good pieces of jasper and agate.

Rockhounding

It is one of those quirks of fate that often determine the course of civilization that made rock collecting possible in this pass. In fact, it was mostly due to the fact that in the winter of 1873 there was no dentist in Silverton, Colorado. It was in that year and in that town that army topographer William L. Marshall had a toothache so severe that his jaws were swollen shut. The nearest dentist was in Denver, and the best route was over Cochetopa Pass. Unfortunately, this pass was often snowed in. The young topographer remembered a possibility on the Continental Divide, so he and Dave Mears—a packer with the army survey team—started out in search of a lower pass. They discovered what was to become Marshall Pass and made it to Denver and the dentist.

As soon as the existence of an easier pass was known, Otto Mears, the famed "Pathfinder of the San Juans," built a road over it. Within 10 years, the pass was a part of the Denver and Rio Grande's narrow-gauge line between Colorado and Utah. Nothing much but rotting ties remains of this old railroad, but in the building of it they did uncover some rocky treasures.

The agate and jasper up here is not large or especially plentiful, but it is here, and there are some nice pieces. We found one very nice little geode filled with clear quartz crystals, but we don't promise that it had any relatives. At the top of the old loading chute, there is a large quantity of very nice white feldspar with embedded gray quartz crystals. Do plan to spend some time in this historic place. Continue through the cut and around to the other side of the hill, where the view toward Gunnison is well worth seeing. There is a lot of old roadbed on this side to explore, too.

Site 62

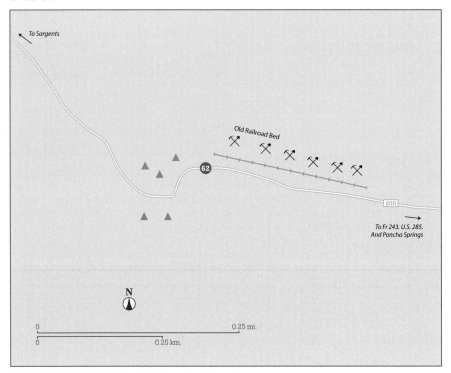

63. Leadville Mines

Looking down from Freemont Pass toward Leadville.

Land type: Mountains.
Elevation: 10,100 feet (at Leadville).
GPS: N39 15.061' / W106 17.617'
Best season: Summer.
Land manager: BLM, San Isabel National Forest Service, and private.
Material: Mineral specimens.
Tools: Rock hammer and small digging tools.
Vehicle: Any to four-wheel drive.
Accommodations: Motels and RV parks in Leadville; and camping in national forest.
Special attractions: Several museums in Leadville. One of the museums in Leadville that you don't want to miss is the mining museum. There is a charge to visit this museum, but it is well worth your time to learn about Colorado mining in the area of Leadville and the surrounding areas.
Finding the site: From I-70, go 5 miles west of Vail, go south on US 24 for 32 miles to Leadville.

Rockhounding

Although the Leadville Mining District is only 20 square miles, it was one of the richest in all of Colorado. A rather humble beginning had miners staking their futures on lead, but this metal was quickly overshadowed by the discovery of a rich lead–silver sulfide ore body. The silver finds kept coming, and by the late 1880s, Leadville was the largest city between St. Louis and San Francisco. The population reached 30,000, and 10 million ounces of silver were produced each year by the 400 working mines in the district. Rockhounds will be interested to know that samples of more than 100 minerals have been found at Leadville. These include, in addition to gold and silver, chrysocolla, azurite, malachite, pyrite, galena, calcite quartz, barite, fluorite, and rhodochrosite. To help find places to go, find the Rock Hut which is a rock and gem business on Harrison Road in the middle of Leadville. This business is owned by Jim and Irene Witmer, and they can help you find places to hunt and explore around Leadville. While you are at the Rock Hut, be sure to take some time to look around their shop as they have many interesting and unique items.

Those who would like to go it alone can head east on CR 2, Seventh Street, or Fifth Street and start looking for likely tailings piles and dumps with no "Keep Out" signs.

Site 63

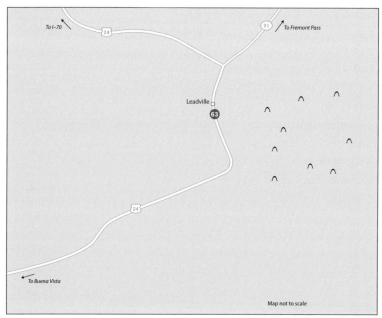

64. Lake City Mines

One of the many mine shaft entrances at Lake City Mines.

Land type: Mountains.
Elevation: 9,193 feet at Henson.
GPS: N38 01.288' / W107 22.722'
Best season: Summer.
Land manager: BLM, Uncompahgre National Forest, and private.
Material: Mineral specimens.
Tools: Rock hammer, small digging tools, and screens.
Vehicle: Any to four-wheel drive.
Accommodations: Bed-and-breakfasts, cabins, lodges, motels, and campgrounds in and around Lake City.
Special attractions: Lake City Museum and ghost towns.
Finding the site: From Gunnison, drive south on CO 149 for approximately 55 miles to Lake City. From Creede, drive northwest for about 50 miles to Lake City. To find the mines, drive west on Hinsdale County Road 20 toward Capitol City. After about 4 miles, you will see mines on the right, near the ghost town of Henson.

About 5 more miles down on CR 20 there are more mines near Capitol City. Or drive southwest on Hinsdale County Road 30 toward Sherman for 20 miles or so to many more old mines. GPS reading was taken at the old town of Henson.

Rockhounding

Lake City is a quiet little town midway between Gunnison and Creede on CO 149. In the 1800s, though, it was a busy transportation center for the freight and passenger traffic to and from the communities that had built up around the San Juan mines. Today, it is remembered less for its place in the mining history of Colorado than for the cannibalistic inclinations of Alferd Packer.

In 1874, Packer was hired as a guide by five prospectors heading into the San Juans. After several weeks, he showed up at the Los Piños Indian Agency and claimed to have lost his charges. After Packer disappeared, search parties found the five men. Four of them had been killed with an ax, and the fifth had been shot. All of them had been butchered and cannibalized. Nine years later, Packer was captured and tried in the Lake City courthouse. Although he was sentenced to death, the sentence was commuted to a prison term from which he was pardoned several years later.

The freight wagons are gone, the mines are shut down, and Packer and his ill-fated clients have passed into the dust of history, but the mine dumps and tailings piles still beckon to the rockhound. The areas to the west and southwest of Lake City are dotted with them. Some of the minerals reported here are quartz crystals, barite, fluorite, calcite, rhodochrosite, pyrite, galena, malachite, and azurite.

Lake City mining area.

Site 64

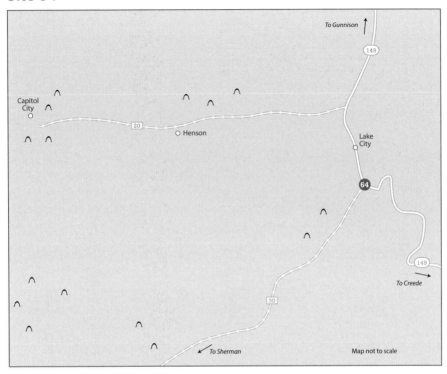

Old buildings still stand at the mines.

65. Bonanza

Milling house and tailing at Bonanza Mine.

Land type: Mountains.
Elevation: 9,451 feet at townsite.
GPS: N38 17.659' / W106 08.563'
Elevation: 9,715 feet at mine site.
GPS: N38 18.779' / W106 09.031'
Best season: Spring through fall.
Land manager: Rio Grande National Forest and private claims.
Material: Pyrite, chrysocolla, and quartz.
Tools: Rock hammer.
Vehicle: Any.
Accommodations: Motels, RV parking, and camping in the Salida area.
Special attractions: Many old mines.
Finding the site: From the intersection of US 50 and US 285 in Poncha Springs, go south on US 285 for 21.6 miles to the junction of Saguache County Road LL56 in Villa Grove. Follow CR LL56 west for 15 miles to center of Bonanza. There are old

mines and mills on both ends of town to search. At the fork, follow the road for 1.4 miles to the mine.

Rockhounding

As you enter the town of Bonanza, you will see some old buildings and foundation ruins on your left across the stream. There are some fairly nice pyrite samples at the top of the old foundation. Continue through the town and hunt in the old mines along the right side of the road. On the dumps, you will find a lot of deep blue to almost purple quartz containing tiny flecks of pyrite. It is vein material and similar to that in which most of the gold in the Colorado mineral belt was found. Gold! Well, who knows?

Site 65

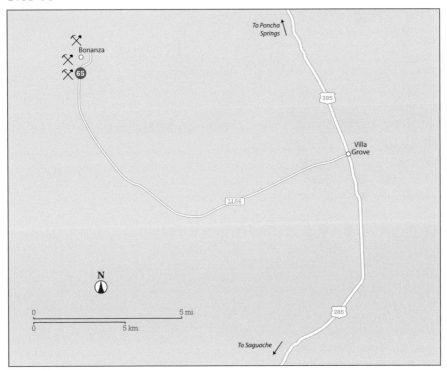

66. Swissvale

These rocks all contain fossils.

Land type: Small canyon.
Elevation: 6,700 feet.
GPS: N38 29.887' / W105 54.400'
Best season: Spring through fall.
Land manager: BLM.
Material: Fossils.
Tools: Rock hammer.
Vehicle: Any.
Accommodations: Motels, RV parking, and camping in the Salida area.
Special attractions: None.
Finding the site: This site will be much easier to find if you have a navigator to keep an eye out for landmarks. It is just off US 50, but it is a little hard to see at 55 mph (or more). From the east side of Salida, drive about 3 miles east on US 50. Look for the Chaffee County/Fremont County border sign. From the sign, the site is exactly 3 miles. Look for a small culvert on the right and a long, wide parking

area on the left side of the highway. If traffic will not allow you to turn around and park on the north side of the road, go on to Swissvale, which is a little less than 1 mile farther. Turn around and look for the antiques shop. Check your odometer and go west 0.6 mile and pull off onto the wide parking area. The culvert is directly across the road. If you still don't spot the culvert, walk over next to the river and look for a concrete culvert running under the highway. This is the outlet, and you might even be able to climb down and walk through it to avoid crossing the highway on foot. When you reach the culvert on the south side of the highway, walk up the little canyon and look for fossils on the hillsides and in the rocks.

Rockhounding

The fossils here are brachiopods in a gray siltstone. They are not big, but are very finely detailed. If you find a particularly good specimen, take as much of the matrix with you as necessary and trim it at home where you have the proper tools. We learned that by sad experience. Getting overeager and watching a great specimen split in half gives you one of those feelings you don't want to repeat.

Site 66

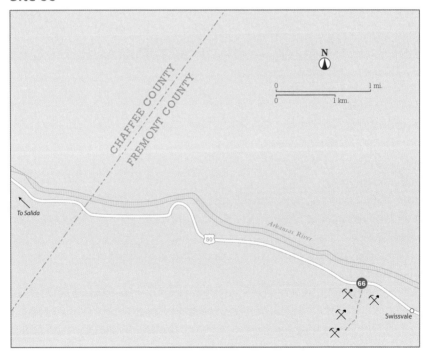

67. Texas Creek

At the parking area. This road leads to the mine.

Land type: Wide wash.
Elevation: 6,355 feet.
GPS: N38 24.966′ / W105 35.217′
Best season: Spring through fall.
Land manager: BLM.
Material: Pink feldspar, mica, and quartz.
Tools: Rock hammer.
Vehicle: Any.
Accommodations: Motels, RV parking, and campgrounds in Salida and Cañon City.
Special attraction: Royal Gorge.
Finding the site: The Texas Creek store is 30 miles east of Salida and 26 miles west of Cañon City on US 50. At the store, zero your odometer and go north across the little bridge over the Arkansas River, across the railroad tracks, and past the cattle guard. Keeping left, keep on the main dirt road, and when you have gone

2 miles, find a place to park and start wandering. The material is everywhere.

Rockhounding

Feldspar, quartz, and mica are plentiful. Texas Creek has been known for its beautiful rose quartz, but the mine, a few miles up the mountain, has been closed to collecting for a long time. We talked to one of the owners, and it doesn't sound like it

A nice rose quartz piece found at Texas Creek.

will be available in the foreseeable future. You never know about those things, though, so if you are up there, make some inquiries. You might get lucky.

Site 67

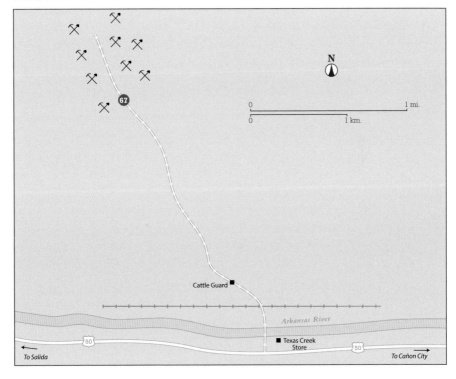

68. Lone Pine Recreation Site

Pink feldspar and agate.

Land type: Riverbank.
Elevation: 6,290 feet.
GPS: N38 23.452' / W105 39.140'
Best season: Spring through fall.
Land manager: BLM.
Material: Feldspar.
Tools: Rock hammer.
Vehicle: Any.
Accommodations: Motels, RV parking, and campgrounds in Salida and Cañon City.
Special attraction: Royal Gorge.
Finding the site: The recreation site is located between US 50 and the Arkansas River, roughly midway between Salida and Cañon City. It is 11.5 miles east of Howard and just 1.8 miles east of the El Carma Rock Shop.

Rockhounding

The rockhounding here is not spectacular, but if you have been driving for hours, you will welcome the chance to stretch your legs, let the kids run off some energy, maybe see some kayakers or rafters, pick up a few pieces of pink feldspar, and, oh yes, use those beautiful restrooms.

Parking area at Lone Pine Recreation Site.

Site 68

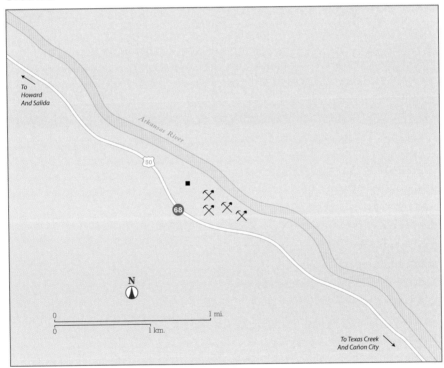

69. Silver Cliff

This area has mines and potholes where others have dug—be careful when you walk and hunt.

Land type: Rolling hills.
Elevation: 7,881 feet.
GPS: N38 08.346' / W105 26.841'
Best season: Summer.
Land manager: BLM and private.
Material: Mineral specimens.
Tools: Rock hammer and digging tools.
Vehicle: High-clearance.
Accommodations: Motels, RV parking, and campgrounds in Westcliffe.
Special attraction: Royal Gorge.
Finding the site: From US 50 at Texas Creek, go south on CO 69 for 25 miles to Westcliffe. At Westcliffe, go east on CO 96 for 1 mile to Silver Cliff. You will see mines and prospect holes all over the White Hills area north of town. Find any road heading out there and get ready to hunt.

Rockhounding

We believe that the hills are BLM land, but are not sure. There is a large mine near the town that is fenced and posted, but nothing else seems to be. It is a well-used area, but if you come across postings, be sure to obey the signs.

Silver was discovered in the area about 1872, and Silver Cliff appeared in 1878 after horn silver was discovered in the White Hills. The mine dumps of the White Hills mines have yielded galena, azurite, malachite, cerussite, argenite, pyrite, and small specimens of horn silver. We didn't find much, but we had just started when Bill backed up from a small dump we had been exploring and hit a small rusty pole sticking out of the ground. After that, we lost the excitement of hunting. We were able to pull the fender back far enough to get the driver's door open and closed, and when we got home the insurance company was thrilled to donate $1,200 to fix it. You have been warned.

Site 69

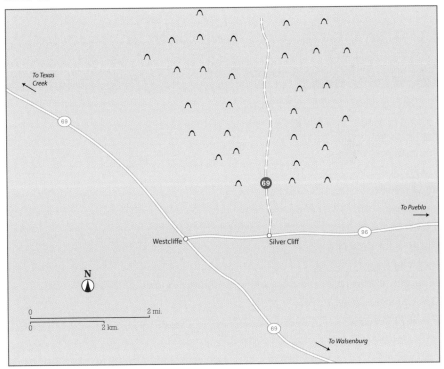

70. Border Feldspar Mine

This gully has nice pink feldspar and mica.

Land type: Mountains.
Elevation: 6,540 feet.
GPS: N38 28.448' / W105 18.453'
Best season: Spring through fall.
Land manager: BLM and Royal Gorge Park.
Material: Feldspar, mica, black tourmaline, and quartz.
Tools: Rock hammer.
Vehicle: Any.
Accommodations: Motels, RV parking, and camping in the Cañon City area.
Special attraction: Royal Gorge.
Finding the site: From Cañon City, go 8 miles west on US 50 to the intersection with Fremont County Road 3A. Follow CR 3A south toward Royal Gorge. At just more than 2.5 miles, you will come to a large sign stating that you are entering Royal Gorge Park. Immediately past this sign turn into the parking area. This is actually part of the old road and loading area for the mine. Huge boulders of

feldspar and mica are used to block the road. A sign warns you to take care not to fall off the mountain while looking around. Walk down the road about 200 yards to the mine itself. The road to the mine is paved with feldspar and mica.

Rockhounding

This site has been hunted for years and years, but it is one of those places that never seems to run out of material. Although you will find all of the feldspar and mica you can stand, there is also black tourmaline in a pure white matrix. These pieces make really nice displays.

While you are in the area, be sure to visit the Royal Gorge and see the world-famous suspension bridge, hanging 1,200 feet above the railway line in the canyon below.

Site 70

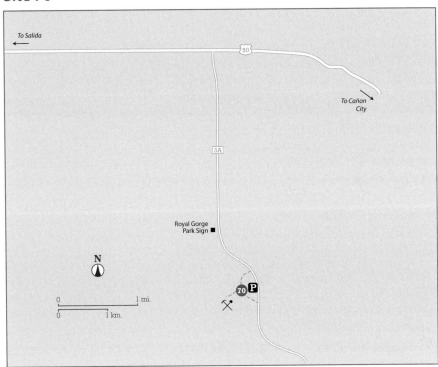

71. Royal Gorge Road

Overlooking the Royal Gorge.

Land type: Hills.
Elevation: 6,642 feet.
GPS: N38 28.216' / W105 18.596'
Best season: Spring through fall.
Land manager: BLM and Royal Gorge Park.
Material: Feldspar, mica, and quartz.
Tools: Rock hammer.
Vehicle: Any.
Accommodations: Motels, RV parking, and campgrounds in Cañon City.
Special attraction: Royal Gorge.
Finding the site: The site is on Royal Gorge Road (CR 3A), just 1 mile from the park gate. Park on the outside of the horseshoe turn, cross the road, and hunt on the low hillside.

Rockhounding

There is a lot of loose material all over the ground at this site. It is nice, but doesn't contain tourmaline needles like those at the Border Feldspar Mine (Site 70). It is so close to the road, however, that if you are on your way to or from the park and don't want to do any walking, you might as well stop and pick up a few souvenirs.

The bend on the road to Royal Gorge has pink feldspar and mica.

Site 71

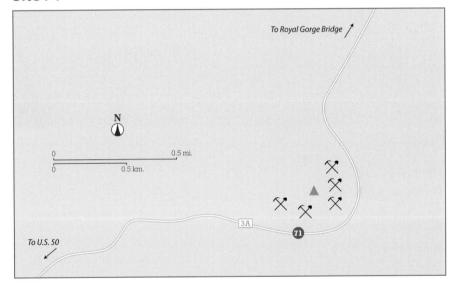

72. Cañon City

Marsh Quarry.

Land type: High desert.
Elevation: 5,836 feet.
GPS: N38 32.103' / W105 13.298'
Best season: Spring through fall.
Land manager: BLM.
Material: Picture stone.
Tools: Rock hammer.
Vehicle: Any.
Accommodations: Motels, RV parking, and camping in the Cañon City area.
Special attraction: Garden Park Research Area.
Finding the site: From US 50 at the east end of Cañon City, go north on Raynolds Avenue for one block. Turn left and proceed west about a tenth of a mile to Field Avenue. Turn right onto Field Avenue and drive 5.7 miles. This road joins on with Red Canyon Road to Marsh Quarry Trail. A dirt track goes up the hill to your left.

Follow it for a quarter mile or so. Here you will come upon a little flat area. Park and search the flat and the low, sandy hills.

Rockhounding

There is quite a bit of sandstone throughout this area that will yield good "pictures." You may have to use your imagination on some of it, but as usual a little persis-

Marsh Quarry trailhead.

tence will turn up some good pieces. There is an orange marble reported in this area, too, but we didn't find any.

The reason for coming to this area used to be to find the famous red and yellow jasper dinosaur bone in what is now the Garden Park Research Area. All of the areas around Garden Park where bone was found are now off-limits to collectors. Oh, to have been a rockhound 40 years ago!

Collecting may be out of the question now, but tours of the digs can be arranged through the BLM from May through September. It would be well worth your effort to see the area where Charles Felch first discovered the dinosaur bones in 1876. So huge were the specimens that he thought they were petrified tree trunks. Since that first discovery, fossils of fish, turtles, mammals, and crocodiles, as well as dinosaurs have been excavated. Even though well over one hundred years have passed since the first discoveries, new sites are found all the time. In July 1994, a new dinosaur egg nest site was discovered 75 feet above one that had been discovered just the year before. That one was determined to be the world's oldest egg site—roughly 150 million years. Also found here was the imprint of a baby dinosaur about a foot long and thought to be only a few days old when it died.

If all of this sounds intriguing, contact the BLM office in Cañon City (see Appendix C) for more information about the area and the tours.

Site 72

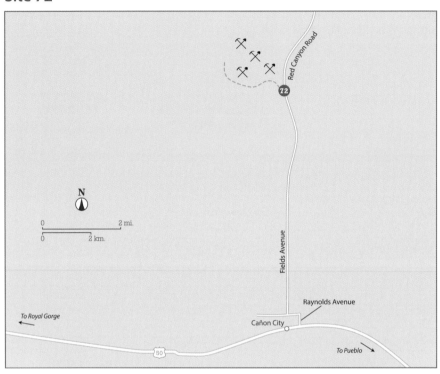

Garden park information at Marsh Quarry.

73. Burnt Mill Road Exit

Small clam shell fossils are found here.

Land type: Roadcut.
Elevation: 5,005 feet.
GPS: N38 07.698' / W104 40.278'
Best season: Spring through fall.
Land manager: Pueblo County Highway Department.
Material: Fossils.
Tools: Rock hammer, small digging tools, and splitting chisel.
Vehicle: Any.
Accommodations: Motels, RV parking, and campgrounds in Pueblo.
Special attractions: None.
Finding the site: From Pueblo, head south on I-25 to exit 88. At the bottom of the off-ramp, turn right and park on the wide pullout area. The fossils await in the low roadcut just across the road to the south.

Rockhounding

This is an easy site to get to, has ample material, and won't take any back-breaking labor to fill up your rock bag. The fossil shells are mostly small clams and oysters, and most are broken, but as usual patience will pay off. There are bits of shell, shells in matrix, and some interesting casts that look almost like pieces of a beehive.

If you wish, you can continue down the road heading west and search both sides along the way. In just over 2 miles, you will come to the junction with Little Burnt Mill Road. You can hunt along Little Burnt Mill Road in either direction for the same fossil material. It is there, but we found the spot back by the interstate to be the best.

Site 73

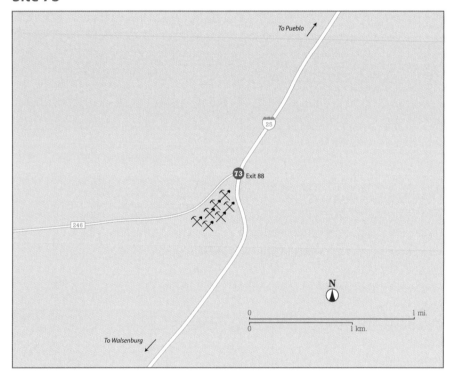

74. Highway 96 (A)

Slag glass found at Highway 96 (A and B) (Sites 74 and 75).

Land type: Plains.
Elevation: 4,322 feet.
GPS: N38 17.693' / W103 22.452'
Best season: Spring through fall.
Land manager: Colorado State Highway Department.
Material: Slag glass.
Tools: Rock hammer.
Vehicle: Any.
Accommodations: This is one of those places where you can say that it may not be the end of the world, but you can see it from here. It is 80 miles from Pueblo to Arlington and 115 miles from Pueblo to Eads, where there is one motel. Motels, RV parking, and campgrounds are available in Pueblo.
Special attractions: None.
Finding the site: From Pueblo, go east on US 50 (Business Loop) to the junction with CO 96. Go left on CO 96 for 57.5 miles. The site is at a break in the big dirt

berm on the north side of the highway. A dirt road leads through the berm and under some large power lines. If you come to Arlington (one house), you have gone too far. Turn around and go back 3.4 miles to the site.

Rockhounding

This site and the next one were so different and so interesting that we just had to include them in the book. We were out crisscrossing the plains, checking washes, roadcuts, and the like to see what we could find. It wasn't much, but we were curious about the huge dirt berm on the north side of the railroad tracks that parallel the highway. It goes on for miles and miles with only an occasional break for a dirt road. We called the chamber of commerce in Eads and were told that the berm is a windbreak for the railroad, to keep the blowing dust and snow from covering the tracks.

We pulled off onto a dirt road and went under the power lines to the north side of the berm. We got out and looked around, and immediately began finding black nodules that we thought were obsidian. They were on top of the berm, all around the berm, on the dirt road, and even in the ballast at the railroad tracks. At the latter find, a lightbulb finally went off in our heads. Did the railroad really use obsidian for ballast? Well, they used what we had been finding, but it wasn't obsidian. See Site 75 for all the details.

A long way from nowhere.

Sites 74-75

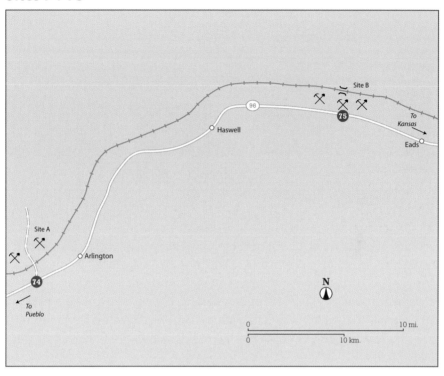

Site B

96

Haswell

75

To
Kansas

Eads

Site A

Arlington

74

To
Pueblo

N

0   10 mi.
0   10 km.

75. Highway 96 (B)

Larry and Marsha Christophersen picking up slag glass.

See map on page 191.

Land type: Plains.

Elevation: 4,124 feet.

GPS: N38 30.117' / W103 00.723'

Best season: Spring through fall.

Land manager: Colorado State Highway Department.

Material: Slag glass.

Tools: Rock hammer.

Vehicle: Any.

Accommodations: Motel in Eads; and motels, RV parking, and campgrounds in Pueblo.

Special attractions: None.

Finding the site: From Highway 96 (A) (Site 74), continue east on CO 96 for 16.6 miles to Haswell. Check your odometer at Haswell and continue on CO 96 for another 9.1 miles. At this point, you will see a railroad bridge over a wash on the north side of the highway. Keep a sharp eye out, since the bridge is at highway level and is a little hard to see. Park off the road and walk over to the site.

Rockhounding

There is much more material here than at Highway 96 (A) (Site 74), and it is quite different. At first we thought we had found obsidian, but there were a lot of multicolored pieces, and the colors just didn't seem right. Still, we had hopes. Have you noticed that when you want something to be, you can convince yourself that it is? Unfortunately we were pretty sure, in the back of our minds, that what we had was slag glass, but we couldn't let go until the good folks at our local community college back home put the last nail in our obsidian coffin. Slag glass is the extra, unused glass that remains at the end of a job at a glass factory. It is usually dumped on the ground to cool. We are not sure how the railway came to use it here.

Don't despair, though. If you find yourself out on this lonely stretch of road, stop and pick up a few pieces of the stuff. You really can cut some interesting cabs with it. Maybe you can even fool Aunt Mabel or Uncle Fred.

Caution: Don't collect the ballast on the railroad tracks. You don't want to be responsible for weakening the track structure, and you don't want to get smacked by a train, either. There is plenty of material down in the wash and under the bridge.

Slag glass from Site 75.

76. Tepee Buttes

Tepee Buttes.

Land type: High plains.
Elevation: 4,775 feet.
GPS: N38 57.413' / W103 11.510'
Best season: Spring through fall.
Land manager: We were told that this was public land, but we saw no postings or signs of any kind. This area is now fenced for the last 0.5 miles.
Material: Fossils.
Tools: Rock hammer and splitting chisel.
Vehicle: Any.
Accommodations: Motels, RV parking, and campgrounds in Limon.
Special attractions: None.
Finding the site: From the junction of CO 94 and US 40/287, go north on US 40/287 for 9.3 miles to Lincoln County Road 2J. Go right on CR 2J for 2.7 miles. At this point, you will see several tepee buttes to the south, with tracks leading out to the Buttes. Park off the road and walk to the buttes.

Rockhounding

These little fossil-filled limestone hills were once reefs at the bottom of the warm, shallow sea that covered most of eastern Colorado about 80 million years ago. As a result of uplifting and deposition, they became pockets in the Pierre Shale that covers much of the area. The shale, being softer, has eroded away, leaving the harder limestone showing as small buttes. The buttes are packed with clam fossils, but you will have to do a bit of digging and splitting to find nice whole ones. There is something here for everyone, though. There are lots of loose pieces and an occasional whole one for those who don't want to dig, and there are some that respond to a tap of the rock hammer for those who are willing to work just a bit. Of course, there is a lot of room for heavy-duty diggers, too. We suggest that you fill in the holes you created before you leave, though. This is open range, and cattle—not being the brightest lights on the string—just might step in and break a leg. Things like that can cause "Keep Out" signs to spring up overnight.

Site 76

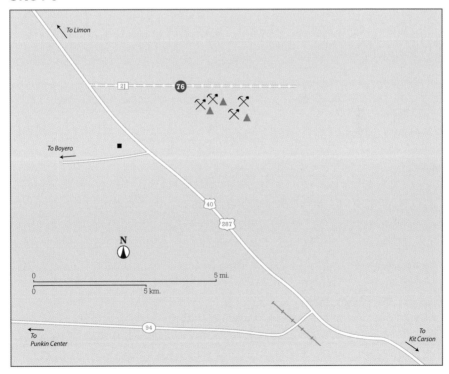

77. Penrose

This area contains calcite crystals on the hills and in the gully.

Land type: Low hills.
Elevation: 5,129 feet.
GPS: N38 24.296' / W105 03.400'
Best season: Spring through fall.
Land manager: BLM.
Material: Calcite crystals.
Tools: Rock hammer.
Vehicle: Any.
Accommodations: Motels, RV parking, and camping in the Cañon City and areas around Pueblo.
Special attractions: None.
Finding the site: From Cañon City, drive east on US 50 for about 30 miles to the Penrose turnoff at CO 115. Turn south onto CO 115 and drive for just over 1 mile. You will see a pullout on the right where you can park. Go through the obvious

opening in the highway fence and walk along the top of the big gully. We found material to the southwest along the hillsides and in the little gullies.

Note: The BLM manages eighty acres here that start about 200 feet from the highway. Technically, this means that you will be crossing private property to get to the calcite crystals. It is obvious that many rockhounds have made the trip, and there is no posting of any kind, so we concluded that it is okay. You might want to make a local inquiry or check with the BLM for the latest information.

Rockhounding

There are some nice calcite crystals at this site. They occur both singly and in clusters, and some are fairly large. You can pick up all you will ever need right off the ground, but if you are willing to split some rock, you might find a real treasure. You can also dig for better samples. The digging is very easy in the soft sand. It is almost like digging at the beach.

Site 77

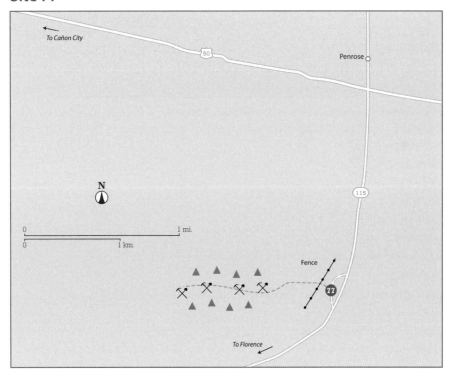

78. Russell

This cut holds brachiopod and gastropod fossils in the shale.

Land type: Roadcut.
Elevation: 8,532 feet.
GPS: N37 34.251′ / W105 16.651′
Best season: Spring through fall.
Land manager: Colorado Department of Transportation.
Material: Fossils.
Tools: Rock hammer and small digging tools.
Vehicle: Any.
Accommodations: Motels, RV parking, and camping in the Alamosa and Walsenburg areas.
Special attractions: None.
Finding the site: From Fort Garland, go east on US 160 for about 12 miles to the small abandoned town of Russell, which is marked by a sign. It is also easy to identify Russell by the "igloo" on the north side of the road at the north end of

town, which may be a highway department building. Whatever it is, go 1 mile northeast of the igloo on US 160. There is an old log cabin down off the road to the left. Immediately past the cabin is a large roadcut. This is your target. Park on the wide shoulder and walk (run) across the highway to the roadcut.

Check the shale for fossils in this cut.

Rockhounding

There are lots of small, but nicely detailed, brachiopod and gastropod fossils in the shale of the cut. Use care, wrap them well, and you will have some nice display pieces when you get home.

Site 78

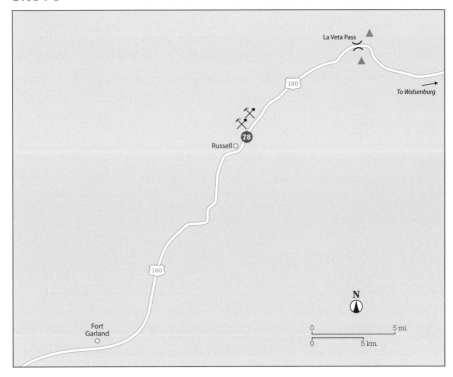

79. St. Peter's Dome

Parking area for St. Peter's Dome.

Land type: Mountains.
Elevation: 9,277 feet.
GPS: N38 44.339' / W104 54.638'
Best season: Spring through fall.
Land manager: Pike National Forest.
Material: Fluorite and feldspar.
Tools: Rock hammer.
Vehicle: Any.
Accommodations: Motels, RV parking, and camping in Colorado Springs.
Special attractions: Garden of the Gods, Pikes Peak, and US Air Force Academy.
Finding the site: The hardest part of finding this site is maneuvering through Colorado Springs to Old Stage Road. There are several ways to get there, and you may want to check out a local city map for a quicker way from your location. The following route will get you there, however. From I-25 take exit 141 (US 24) west to the intersection of 21st Street. Drive south on 21st Street for about 4.5 miles.

Don't be confused by the street name: 21st Street becomes Cresta Road, Cresta Road becomes El Pomar Road, and El Pomar becomes Penrose Boulevard. It is all the same street, though, so press on. Penrose Boulevard crosses Old Stage Road just before the entrance to the Cheyenne

This road takes you over to the old railroad tunnel.

Mountain Zoo. Do not continue on to the zoo, but take Old Stage Road west. At 0.7 mile, the pavement ends and a good forest road winds upward through private property for another 7 miles. At this point, you will see a pullout for a viewpoint and the trailhead to St. Peter's Dome. To the right of the pullout, a dirt road leads to a shooting range. Follow this road for 0.3 mile and park by the huge boulders that have been set up to block the road. Walk beyond the boulders and hunt on all of the hills. If you continue down the old road, you will come to one of the tunnels on the old Gold Camp Road. These were originally railroad tunnels on the narrow-gauge railroad that connected Colorado Springs with Cripple Creek. After the railroad was abandoned, the tracks were torn up, and the roadbed became an automobile road. In 1988, the tunnels were declared unsafe, and the road was closed.

Rockhounding

Purple, white, and green fluorite is abundant all over the area. Seams and outcrops are found in the hillsides, and dumps are a good source. If you are up to hiking, the areas beyond the tunnel and below the road are reported to have additional material. There have also been reports that zircon may still be found in the dumps of the old mine below the road.

Site 79

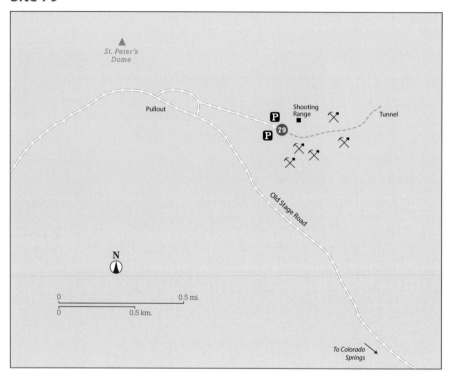

St. Peter's Dome

Pullout

Shooting Range

Tunnel

79

Old Stage Road

N

| 0 | | 0.5 mi. |

| 0 | | 0.5 km. |

To Colorado Springs

80. Devils Head

White quartz and feldspar along with topaz are found in this area.

Land type: Mountains.
Elevation: 8,955 feet.
GPS: N39 16.201' / W105 06.286'
Best season: Spring through fall.
Land manager: Pike National Forest.
Material: Microcline orthoclase, quartz, black tourmaline, graphic granite, and topaz.
Tools: Rock hammer and small digging tools.
Vehicle: Any.
Accommodations: Motels, RV parking, and camping in the Denver and Colorado Springs areas.
Special attraction: US Air Force Academy.
Finding the site: Leave I-25 south of Denver near Castle Rock at exit 183. Go west on US 85 for 7 miles to Sedalia. At Sedalia, take CO 67 southwest for 10 miles to the junction with Rampart Range Road. Turn left on Rampart Range Road and

follow it for 10.4 miles to Devils Head turnoff. This area is now a large Forest Service attraction. Make sure that you check regulations before hunting in this area.

Rockhounding

Walk along the road through the pines and look for the white quartz and pink feldspar outcroppings. Old digging sites are easily spotted and some nice material can be found. This is an old collecting area, and although the huge crystals that have been found here seem to be a thing of the past, there is still plenty of nice material to collect.

The area was noted for smoky quartz and topaz crystals as well as amazonite. We found some fine microcline orthoclase with white quartz and black tourmaline, and nice graphic granite. There are so many digging sites and so much more granite to be broken up and screened that we have no doubt that time, persistence, and boulder breaking will turn up some smoky quartz and probably some topaz.

Site 80

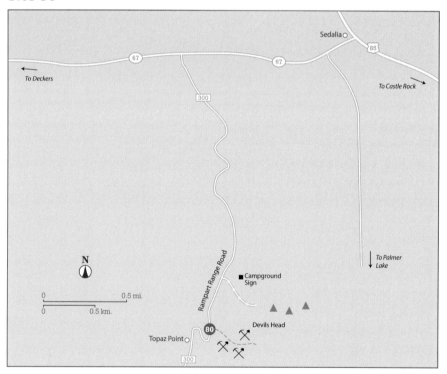

81. Perry Park

A nice piece of alabaster at this site.

Land type: Roadcut.
Elevation: 6,586 feet.
GPS: N39 15.545' / W104 59.030'
Best season: Spring through fall.
Land manager: Douglas County Road Department.
Material: Fossils, alabaster, and satin spar.
Tools: Rock hammer.
Vehicle: Any.
Accommodations: Motels, RV parking, and camping in the Denver and Colorado Springs areas.
Special attractions: None.
Finding the site: This trip begins at Sedalia on US 85, south of Denver and west of I-25. Take exit I-25 to US 85 and proceed 7 miles to Sedalia. At Sedalia, turn south onto CO 105 toward Palmer Lake. At 14.4 miles, take Red Rock Road west for 1.8 miles to Perry Park Road. Turn right and go less than 0.5 mile to the high roadcut

across from the golf course. Pull off the road and park. This area is now a housing development with private drives and land.

Rockhounding

This roadcut has numerous seams and outcroppings of both alabaster and satin spar. The satin spar is especially nice. You can pick up good samples along the base of the cut; but for the best material, find a likely seam, clear away the soft sand, and break off nice solid pieces.

Fossils of both leaves and marine lives are reported in the sandstone northwest of the golf course, but we didn't get over there to check. Maybe you will have some luck there.

Site 81

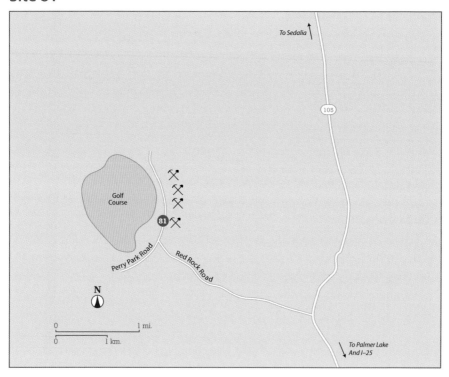

FIFTEEN TRIPS FOR THE INTREPID EXPLORER

These fifteen trips are for those who buy grab bags at the county fair or who never fail to get a lottery ticket each week. There may be treasures waiting, or there may be only sore feet, sunburn, and the frustration of "private property" signs. I have included them for the following two reasons. First, the site may be one we have visited and found nothing, but feel that there is material for someone who will spend the time to hunt and dig. These are all places we have promised ourselves to revisit as soon as we have the time. Second, there are those sites that are on our list of places to go as soon as we get around to it. Maybe you will beat us there and get all of the good stuff.

All of these sites should be good possibilities, but no warranties are expressed or implied. They may be posted as private property, they may have shopping malls built on top of them, or they may be collected out. In addition, remember that in the case of the sites I haven't visited, directions may be fuzzy or downright inaccurate. If you are a grab-bag or lottery ticket buyer, get your bag and hammer and go for it.

CORTEZ AREA (GPS N37 20'57.09" / W108 35'10.73")

About the site: This is an area we have been around a lot but haven't explored for its potential. There are reports of agate and jasper in the area, and dinosaur bone has been found near Hovenweep National Monument. All we ever found on the road to Hovenweep was a muddy ditch where our truck got stuck, but the material is there for the intrepid explorer. South of Cortez near the town of Towaoc is a mountain that is said to contain agate, jasper, and fossils. Unfortunately, the mountain is on the Ute Mountain Indian Reservation and permission to collect is rarely, if ever, given. Who knows, though, you may request permission on a day when the powers that be are in a magnanimous mood. It sure would be worth a try.

The spot we are most interested in is up McElmo Canyon at Goodman Point, just west of Cortez. The hunting area is on BLM land, but there is a strip of private land that must be crossed to get to it. Local inquiries should determine how friendly the landowners are. San Juan Gems, a large rock shop in Cortez, should be a good source of information about the whole area. They may also be able to help you avoid trespassing on the reservation or collecting in Hovenweep National Monument.

Finding the site: To get to the Goodman Point site, start at the west end of Cortez and go south on US 160/666 for about 3 miles to Montezuma County Road G. Take CR G west for about 7 miles. CR J goes north across a creek. Follow it as far as you can toward the point. GPS reading was taken in the town of Cortez, CO.

TARRYALL AREA (GPS N39 07'29.79" / W105 28'38.63")

About the site: Tarryall is an old mining area and one that has been rockhounded to death. A gentleman in Calhan assured us, however, that there are still nice quartz, topaz, and other mineral and crystal specimens there. If you are in the Lake George and Round Mountain Campground area anyway, give Tarryall a try. You may be richly rewarded.

Finding the site: There are two roads going north to Tarryall from US 24. Head west from Lake George on US 24. At just 0.5 mile, the first Tarryall road heads north. This is Teller County Road 77. Don't turn here, but continue west on US 24 for 5 more miles to the second Tarryall road. I have a conflict on my maps, so this road is either FR 222 or Teller County Road 31. In either case, it is easy to spot. It is a wide dirt road and easily seen from the highway. Take this road north toward Tarryall and watch for mine dumps, piles of tailings, and prospect holes on the left. Explore them all. Good luck! GPS reading was taken near Tarryall.

WOLF CREEK PASS (GPS N37 28'59.39" / W106 48'07.47")

About the site: We have been over Wolf Creek Pass more times than we care to remember. And we have read about, heard about, and been given specific directions to the geode area. When we finally had some time to look around, it was raining. We slogged around and found nothing, but we may be the only rockhounds in Colorado who never had luck here. If you are in the area, give it a try. The geodes are said to be small but very pretty.

Finding the site: From Pagosa Springs, drive about 10 miles north on US 160. You will see the turnoff to Treasure Falls. Check your odometer and go 0.5 mile farther. Park off the highway and hunt along the cliff to the right. Geodes have also been reported on the other side of the highway. Look hard and spend some time. GPS reading was taken at Wolf Creek Pass.

MACK (GPS N39 13'27.01" / W108 51'54.38")

About the site: Beyond the tiny town of Mack, a good dirt road runs along West Salt Creek for 15 or 20 miles. Petrified wood has been reported along here, but we didn't find any. A local oil worker said he had found a little on a hillside while hunting in the area. This is a big area, and there are lots of side roads and tracks to follow. We have a hunch that a lot of time and some work will turn up good specimens. But then again, we have had those hunches before. Are you adventurous?

Finding the site: From Grand Junction, take either I-70 or US 6 west for about 17 miles to Mack. At Mack, take Mesa County Road M.80 west to its junction with CR 8. Go north on CR 8 to its junction with CR S. Take CR S to the west and follow it along West Salt Creek. The directions sound confusing, but the land is flat and it is easy to see where you are going. You would have to work at it to get lost. GPS reading was taken at the freeway exit at Mack.

BOOK CLIFFS (Campgrounds) (GPS N39 16'13.16" / W108 50'13.93")

About the site: The Book Cliffs are barren mountains of gray Mancos shale capped with Mesa Verde sandstone. They stand from 1,000 to 2,000 feet high and run 175 miles from Palisade, Colorado, just east of Grand Junction, to Price, Utah. Although you could probably find rockhounding fun in most of the range, we will confine this trip to the area near Grand Junction. Barite crystals and fossil ammonites have been reported along the cliffs from Palisade northward. There is a lot of area to cover, and it can be hot in the summer, so try to do your collecting in the spring or fall.

Finding the site: The following directions will get you to one spot at the base of the cliffs, but you should use any of the many roads and tracks that head there. You will need some time and patience, but you should be rewarded. Don't overlook talking to local rock shop owners or clubs. You may get specific directions that will put you right down on the Hope Diamond of barite. At the west end of Grand Junction, take Mesa County Road 25 north for about 2.5 miles beyond I-70. Note that you will have to pick up CR 25 in Grand Junction either on US 6 or US 50, or from a side street. There is no access from I-70. At the 2.5-mile point on CR 25, the pavement ends. In another 3 miles or so, the road forks. The map shows only the right fork, but you can take either one. Be aware, also, that the map doesn't show the many other forks and side roads. Don't worry about which ones to take, just keep heading toward the cliffs. On the way, you will pass mounds of shale, which should be checked out, too. GPS reading was taken at the campgrounds in this area.

HAHNS PEAK (GPS N40 48'22.21" / W106 56'40.20")

About the site: Hahns Peak is a 10,820-foot peak north of Steamboat Springs. The top part of the park contains a number of old mines that produced gold, silver, lead, and copper. Of interest to the rockhound are the large quartz crystals for which the area is famous. This is a site we haven't visited, so we can't verify that there are any of those monster crystals that you will have to tie on top of your car to get home. You might well find some very nice smaller ones, though. We also don't know whether the mines are posted to keep people out. The peak is in the Routt National Forest, and that is a good sign. You might want to check with the Forest Service office in Steamboat Springs (see Appendix E) before you make the trip. They should be able to help with the collecting status in the area.

Finding the site: From Steamboat Springs, drive north on Routt County Road 129 for about 20 miles to the town of Hahns Peak. We understand that several Forest Service roads go up the mountain, so local inquiries may save your sanity. GPS reading was taken at Hahns Peak Village. There is a visitor center nearby where you might be able to find directions.

PINKHAM MOUNTAIN (GPS N40 56'10.04" / W106 15'03.38")

About the site: Pinkham Mountain is the site of some massive fluorite and fluorspar veins. Mining on the mountain began in the 1900s and lasted until the 1970s. Some beautiful specimens have been taken from the mines and tailings. At one time, there were fine examples of fluorite with marcasite and pyrite. Unfortunately, there is a lot of private property around the mountain. A friend who has some land west of the area has told us that the mines are probably posted and locked. However, he also said that there is a possibility of obtaining permission to collect. We don't know if this is possible or not, but if you are hunting near Delaney Butte (Site 13), it is only a dozen miles or so to Pinkham Mountain. Maybe it is worth looking at.

Finding the site: From Walden, go north on CO 125 for 12 miles to its junction with CO 127. Turn east onto CO 127, and in 1 mile or so you will see Pinkham Mountain on your left. GPS reading was taken at Pinkham Mountain.

ALTA (GPS N37 53'09.56" / W107 51'15.14")

About the site: Alta was the company town for the Gold King Mine north of Ophir. The original precious metals were discovered in 1877, and the mines in the area operated until after World War II. As would be expected from a town with such a long life span, the buildings are a mix of old log structures and fairly modern houses. All of the log buildings are down now, and the rest are following. The remains of the store crumble a little more each year, and the very photogenic three-story boardinghouse will probably join the rest in the not-too-distant future. The mill, which was at the foot of the town, burned down years ago, but crucibles and other interesting paraphernalia can be found in the rubble. This area is now under claim with very few areas to rockhound in. The site in the book has been taken out because of the private claims everywhere. There are tailings in this area but be sure to make inquiries before you do any rockhounding at this location.

Finding the site: Alta is located off CO 145, north of the turnoff to Ophir and the Ophir Pass Road. Just north of Ophir, take the unmarked road going east for just less than 4 miles to the Alta townsite. The first mile or so of the road is narrow, and part of it crosses a shelf above CO 145. Unless the weather is bad, the family car will make the trip, but it gets very bumpy. A pickup would be better, if you have the choice. GPS reading was taken in the ghost town of Alta, CO.

CHALK CREEK (GPS N38 42'52.48" / W106 13'06.16")

About the site: We have had Chalk Creek on our list of sites to check out for a long time, but something always seemed to keep us away. We finally got a chance, but it was a little late in the year, and the Leadville area decided to have an early snow. Evidently, the weatherman heard we were coming. We wouldn't want you to think we are fair-weather rockhounds—we have hunted in the snow in Utah—but a foot of new snow can cover up a lot of those twinned orthoclase crystals, even if they are supposed to be 2 inches in length. If you can get up there in the summer, give it a try. We have a hunch that you will be rewarded.

Finding the site: CO 91 goes northeast toward Fremont Pass. At about 8.5 miles from Leadville, there is a pullout where Chalk Creek goes under the highway. Park and hike a couple of hundred yards up the rough road to the north and hunt on the hillsides. GPS reading was taken at Chalk Creek.

FLAGLER FOSSILS (GPS N39 17'35.51" / W103 04'01.24")

About the site: We had gone out to the Flagler area looking for fossils for the first edition of this book, but we didn't have any luck. We came across a ranger who told us about the cone-in-cone material at Flagler Lake, and we forgot all about fossils. They are probably still there, though (just a little bit older), so if you are a fossil hunter, or if you are just tired of I-70, get off the highway and onto the frontage road at Flagler and hunt in the gullies on both sides of the road for clams, oysters, and maybe even an ammonite or some shark's teeth. You can also find gullies that are said to contain the same types of fossils as those found off CO 59 north of Seibert.

Finding the site: The area is easy to find. Flagler is just off I-70 about 35 miles east of Limon. CO 59 is about 10 miles farther east. If you find yourself in Kansas, you went too far. GPS reading was taken in the town of Flagler, CO.

KIOWA WOOD (GPS N39 20'47.19" / W104 28'24.81")

About the site: The part of Elbert County around the towns of Kiowa, Elizabeth, and Elbert has been the source of some of the largest petrified logs in Colorado. According to Stephen Voynick in *Colorado Rockhounding,* logs 20 feet long and 2 feet in diameter washed out of the gullies back in the 1940s. All of the gullies south of CO 86 and east and west of Elbert County Roads 25–41 are likely places to look for some colorful treasures. Be sure that you do not trespass, since much of the land is private. Be careful, too, if it looks as though a storm may be coming. Way back in 1878, on May 21, a cloudburst hit the area and sent a wall of water roaring down Kiowa Creek. It struck a freight train of the Kansas Pacific Railway with such force that the bodies of the fireman and the brakeman were not found until the next day—1.5-miles downstream. It was 4 days until the engineer's body was found—10 miles downstream. The story goes that the locomotive was never found.
Finding the site: Look for creeks and gullies crossing CO 86 between Castle Rock and Limon. Take CR 25-41 from Kiowa south toward Colorado Springs and watch for ways to get over to the creek. As usual, a few local inquiries might get you on the right track. GPS reading was taken at the junction of CO 86 and North Elbert Road, just west of the town of Kiowa.

OHIO CITY (GPS N38 34'01.62" / W106 36'42.64")

About the site: Ohio City was like one of those trick birthday cake candles that won't stay blown out. Each time you think you have blown it out, the flame pops back up. In the 1860s, Ohio City (first called Eagle City) came into being as a placer gold mining area. The placers played out, and no one bothered to find the source of the nuggets, so the flame flickered out. The silver boom that started around 1879 saw miners returning to Ohio City, and sure enough, silver was found. The flame flared up, and all was well until the collapse of the silver market in 1893, when it dwindled and went out again. In 1896, some intrepid miners found the source of the 1860s nuggets and the flame burned once again until it petered out around 1916. It's been out a long time now, but maybe you will be the one to start it up again while poking around some of the old mines. There are a number of them in the area, but the most important seems to have been the Willow Creek Mine. It has been hunted for years, but there's still a chance of finding a little feldspar, quartz, muscovite mica, or graphic granite. If you are up there checking out the Opportunity Mine (Site 47), you might as well have a go at the Ohio City area.

Finding the site: Follow the directions to the Opportunity Mine (Site 45). Continue on past the Opportunity Mine for about 4.5 miles and take a dirt road to the left. Just after the turn, there should be a fork to the right that crosses Willow Creek. Continue up this fork to some old mines on the hills to the right of the road. These directions are very old, so if you don't see the mines, just do some exploring in the area. You may be rewarded. It's beautiful country anyway, so eat that picnic lunch, take some pictures, and enjoy. GPS reading was taken in Ohio City. Follow directions from there.

GUNNISON GOLD BELT (GPS N38 19'08.52" / W107 05'55.23")

About the site: In the middle 1890s, a gold strike south of Gunnison had many thinking that the 40-square-mile area that came to be known as the Gunnison Gold Belt would rival the Cripple Creek area. Because ore with the same characteristics was found in both Leadville and Lake City, many miners were eager to make the connection and believed that there was a continuous mineral belt between the two. Camps such as Spencer, Iris, Goose Creek, and Vulcan sprang up, and the search was on for the mother lode. The great hopes never materialized, though. The area did well for a few years, but by the turn of the century it was over. In the early 1900s, a little activity centered on copper mining, but that too went the way of the early mines. Today, the area is mostly ranch land, but old dumps and tailings piles are still there. Mineral specimens are reported to be there for the taking.

Finding the site: To reach the area, go west from Gunnison on US 50 for 7 or 8 miles to the junction with CO 149. Head south for just over 13 miles, where you should see an old wooden structure and a mine dump reported to have specimens of white quartz and some malachite. About 2 miles farther down the road are more dumps and more specimens. To reach the ghost town of Vulcan, GPS N38 20'49.07" / W107 00'07.85", head back toward US 50 to the junction of CO 149 and CR 31. Go south on CR 31 for about 13 miles to Vulcan. The dumps here are from gold and copper mines and might just have some interesting specimens. The GPS reading was taken close to the actual site and not in the town of Gunnison. The GPS reading for Vulcan was taken in the approximate area of where Vulcan used to be. Don't confuse this site with the Vulcan mines found on Highway 170, near the town of New Castle.

TROUT CREEK (GPS N38 54'35.82" / W105 58'31.11")

About the site: A number of years ago, we came across a little booklet that listed some of the more popular collecting areas in Colorado. Tucked in the middle was a site called Chubb Park, down near Buena Vista. Now, we have never cut and polished a Chubb, so we tucked the information away for one of those "someday" trips. (Actually the material specified wasn't Chubb, but agate and opalized wood.) We have been by the area several times, but haven't gone roaming to see if the material is really there. It does look promising from the road, but it will take a fair amount of hiking to get down to the creek. If you have the time, give it a try. Who knows?

Finding the site: This is a very easy site to find. Take US 24 south from Buena Vista for about 2 miles to its junction with US 285. Go left at the junction and follow US 24/285 for about 15 miles toward Trout Creek Pass. When you reach the summit, find a place to turn around and head back toward Buena Vista. The collecting area runs for about 4 miles from the summit toward Buena Vista. The material is supposed to be on the hillside and on down to Chubb Creek and Trout Creek. If you find some good stuff, write and tell us. GPS reading was taken at Trout Creek Pass.

WRAY (GPS N40 04'44.22" / W102 13'39.81")

About the site: Way up in the northeast corner of Colorado, just south of the town of Wray, the Arikaree and Republican Rivers cross under US 385. Along both of these rivers and some of the small tributaries can be found cretaceous marine fossils. These fossils are primarily pelecypods and cephalopods. The gullies in the area are also reported to contain agate, jasper, petrified wood, and opalized wood. This is a long way from anything but Kansas, so do a little phoning before you commit to a long trip. On the other hand, if you are going that way, plan a little stop-off.

Finding the site: Wray is on US 385, 56 miles north of Burlington and 69 miles south of Julesburg. The Arikaree River is about 20 miles south of Wray, and the Republican River is another 15 miles or so south of that. Don't forget the sandwiches. GPS reading was taken in Wray.

APPENDIX A: GLOSSARY

Agate: A form of chalcedony containing bands or mossy inclusions; often very colorful, but sometimes with either one color or very muted colors.

Aggregate: A mixture of different kinds of rocks or crystals.

Alabaster: A fine-grained variety of gypsum used widely for carving.

Amethyst: A gemstone of the quartz family, ranging in color from pale lilac to deep purple.

Ammonite: A cephalopod fossil curled like a ram's horn.

Aquamarine: A form of beryl next in desirability to emerald; colors range from pale to deep blue or blue green.

Aragonite: A form of calcite that often forms in layers or bands and is sometimes mistaken for onyx.

Azurite: A blue copper carbonate often associated with malachite.

Baculite: A cephalopod fossil of the same family as the ammonite, but straight rather than curled.

Barite: Barium sulfate occurring in blue, green, brown, and red colors.

Beryl: Beryllium aluminum sulfate that is colorless in its pure form; varieties include emerald, green; aquamarine, blue; morganite, pink; and heliodor, brown to golden yellow.

Biotite: A member of the mica group usually in black, brown black, or green black.

Book: Term for a common occurrence of mica in leaves that resemble the pages of a book.

Brachiopod: A marine animal with two nearly symmetrical shells, but with one slightly larger than the other.

Cabbing: The act of creating a cabochon.

Cabochon (Cab): A common shape for a gem, usually with an elliptical perimeter and a domed top.

Calcite: Calcium carbonate that occurs in clear as well as white, brown, red, yellow, and blue crystals.

Cephalopod: Free-swimming marine animal; ammonites and baculites are typical of cephalopods.

Chalcedony: A cryptocrystalline form of quartz in which the crystal structure is not visible to the naked eye; forms include agate, jasper, carnelian, sard, onyx, chrysoprase, sardonyx, and flint.

Cleavelandite: A form of albite in the plagioclase feldspar group.

Concretion: A cemented accumulation of mineral material; may contain pyrite, silica, calcite, or gypsum.

Country rock: The common rock surrounding a vein or other deposit of gemstones or minerals.

Crinoid: One of hundreds of round stem-like echinoderms; usually only parts are found as fossils.

Crystal: A solid mineral having a regular geometric shape with flat faces or surfaces.

Dendrite: A mineral inclusion in a rock which resembles the branching of a fern.

Dike: A wall of igneous rock surrounded by country rock.

Epidote: Green crystal sometimes used as a gemstone, but more commonly collected for display.

Feldspar: The most abundant mineral in the Earth's crust; classified as orthoclase and plagioclase; among the most desired varieties are moonstone, sunstone, microcline, and labradorite.

Float: Gemstones or minerals that have been transported from their place of origin by water, erosion, or gravity.

Fluorite: A common mineral that occurs in colors of white, brown, purple, green, yellow, violet, and blue; sometimes faceted, but too soft to stand up to day-to-day wear as jewelry.

Fluorspar: A less pure and more granular form of fluorite.

Fortification agate: Agate with acutely banded corners that form a closed figure resembling a fort.

Fossils: Remains of plants, insects, or animals preserved in casts or molds.

Gangue: Country rock, or other rock of no value, surrounding minerals or gemstones.

Garnet: A group of differently colored but chemically similar minerals. The group includes pyrope, red with brown; almandine, red with violet; spessartite, orange to red brown; grossular, yellow to copper brown; demantoid, emerald green; and uvarovite, emerald green.

Gem: A gemstone that has been prepared for use in jewelry.

Gemstone: Any precious or semiprecious stone that can be cut, polished, and used in jewelry.

Geode: A hollow nodule or concretion, usually filled with crystal formations.

Gypsum: A hydrous calcium sulfate that occurs in white, colorless, gray, brown, red, and yellow; colorless variety is called selenite, and dense form is called alabaster.

Igneous: Rock formed by solidification or crystallization of magma; one of the three primary classifications of rock.

Jasper: Opaque form of chalcedony, often with mossy inclusions or intertwining of various colors.

Lapidary: The art of forming and shaping gemstones; one who forms or shapes gemstones.

Lepidolite: Pink to lilac–colored silicate mineral of the mica group.

Limonite: A term applied generally to a brownish iron hydroxide; often occurs as a pseudomorph after iron minerals such as pyrite.

Malachite: A green copper ore that occurs both in crystal and massive forms. Massive forms are often banded, and many contain beautiful bull's-eyes.

Massive form: The form of a mineral in which the crystals are either very small or without any discernible definition.

Matrix: Material in which a mineral crystal or fossil is embedded.

Metamorphic: Preexisting rock changed by the action of pressure, chemical action, or heat; one of the three primary classifications of rock.

Mica: A group of sheet silicate minerals, major members of which are muscovite, biotite, phlogopite, lepidolite, and chlorite.

Micromount: A tiny mineral specimen intended for viewing under a microscope.

Muscovite: One of the mica group; usually colorless to pale yellow, green, pink, or brown.

Onyx: A black and white–banded chalcedony; colored varieties sold in gift shops are either dyed onyx or a form of calcite or aragonite.

Opal: A silicon oxide closely related to chalcedony, but softer and containing water. Common opal is often dull and not suitable for jewelry, but some have a waxy texture and will cut and polish into nice cabochons. They often replace wood fibers in fossil wood and make finely detailed samples. Precious opal is the type associated with fine jewelry and shows beautiful flashes of multicolored fire; often mistakenly called fire opal, but true fire opal is red and does not have the flashes of fire.

Pegmatite: Coarse-grained igneous rock often the host for gemstones and minerals; usually found as smaller masses in large igneous formations.

Pelecypods: Bivalved mollusks with shells that meet evenly at the hinge; not symmetrical as in the brachiopods; oysters, clams, and mussels are typical pelecypods.

Petrification: The process by which silica or other minerals replace the cell structure of organic material.

Porphyry: Rock containing crystals in a fine-grained mass.

Pseudomorph: A crystal with the geometric appearance of one mineral, but which has been chemically replaced with another mineral.

Pyrite: Iron sulfide or disulfide with a brassy yellow color; commonly called "fool's gold."

Quartz (Cryptocrystalline): A group that includes amethyst, aventurine, citrine, rose quartz, smoky quartz, and tiger eye.

Quartz (Macrocrystalline): A group that includes chalcedony, agate, jasper, onyx, chrysoprase, and sard.

Rhodochrosite: A manganese carbonate gemstone in colors from rose red to white with striping; sometimes forms as stalactites in caves.

Rhodonite: A deep red to pink gemstone usually with black manganese oxide inclusions that often appear as spider webbing.

Sedimentary: Rock formed by deposition, compaction, and cementation; one of the three primary classifications of rock.

Silicafied: A mineral or organic compound that has been replaced by silica.

Tailings: Waste material from mining or milling.

APPENDIX B: MAP SOURCES

The maps in this book coupled with any standard highway map of Colorado will get you to the sites just fine; but if you would like to expand your explorations, you may want to purchase some additional maps. The maps that were used by Gary and Sally in revising this rockhounding book was the *Colorado Road and Recreation Atlas* and is published by Benchmark Maps. It can be found in many bookstores and markets throughout Colorado. This atlas has been field checked for accuracy and in using this atlas, they will tell you that it is accurate for all sites within this book. It was updated in 2012 by Benchmark Books. This atlas has landscape maps, recreation guides, detailed roads, and shows public lands. If you are planning on exploring Colorado, this is one atlas that you should have in your collection. The Forest Service, the BLM, and the US Geological Survey also publish maps that will help you find your way in the backcountry.

Caution: Many of these maps haven't been updated for as much as 20 years. That is not long in geological terms, but it is an eternity in the life of a dirt road or jeep road. Don't be surprised, then, if some of the roads shown on the maps no longer exist or have been closed. Don't be surprised, either, if there are more roads than those shown. If you find unlisted roads, give them a try. You never know what you might find along the way. Someone went to a good deal of trouble to build even the most primitive of roads. He must have had a reason; go find out what it was.

Where to obtain National Forest maps:

Arapaho and Roosevelt National Forests
Forest Supervisor
240 W. Prospect Rd.
Fort Collins, CO 80526-2098
(970) 498-1375

Gunnison, Grand Mesa, and Uncompahgre National Forests
Forest Supervisor
2250 Hwy. 50
Delta, CO 81416
(970) 874-6600

Medicine Bow–Routt National Forest
Forest Supervisor
2468 Jackson St.
Laramie, WY 82070-6535
(307) 745-2300

Pike and San Isabel National Forests
Forest Supervisor
2840 Kachina Dr.
Pueblo, CO 81008
(719) 553-1400

Rio Grande National Forest
1803 W. Hwy. 160
Monte Vista, CO 81144
(719) 852-5941

San Juan National Forest
Supervisor's Office
15 Burnett Ct.
Durango, CO 81301
(970) 247-4874

White River National Forest
Supervisor's Office
PO Box 948
900 Grand Ave.
Glenwood Springs, CO 81602
(970) 945-2521

Bureau of Land Management Maps
US Department of the Interior
Bureau of Land Management
Colorado State Office
2850 Youngfield St.
Lakewood, CO 80215
(303) 239-3600

US Geological Survey Maps
USGS Rocky Mountain Mapping Center
Branch of Information Services
PO Box 25286
Denver, CO 80225
(888) 275-8747

APPENDIX C: BUREAU OF LAND MANAGEMENT CONTACT INFORMATION

State Office
2850 Youngfield St.
Lakewood, CO 80215
(303) 239-3600
fax (303) 239-3933
www.co.blm.gov/csomap.htm

Field Offices:
Grand Junction Field Office
2815 H Rd.
Grand Junction, CO 81506
(970) 244-3000
fax (970) 244-3083
www.co.blm.gov/gjra/gjra.html

Little Snake Field Office
455 Emerson St.
Craig, CO 81625
(970) 826-5000
fax (970) 826-5002
http://www.blm.gov/co/st/en/fo/
lsfo.html

White River Field Office
73544 Hwy. 64
Meeker, CO 81641
(970) 878-3800
fax (970) 878-3805
TDD (970) 878-4227
www.co.blm.gov/wrra/index.htm

Kremmling Field Office
2103 E. Park Ave.
PO Box 68
Kremmling, CO 80459
(970) 724-3000
fax (970) 724-9590
www.co.blm.gov/kra/kraindex.htm

Glenwood Springs Field Office
50629 Hwy. 6 and 24
PO Box 1009
Glenwood Springs, CO 81602
(970) 947-2800
fax (970) 947-2829
www.co.blm.gov/gsra/gshome.htm

Uncompahgre Field Office
2505 S. Townsend Ave.
Montrose, CO 81401
(970) 240-5300
fax (970) 240-5367
www.co.blm.gov/ubra/index.html

Gunnison Field Office
216 N. Colorado St.
Gunnison, CO 81230
(970) 641-0471
fax (970) 641-1928
www.co.blm.gov/gra/index.html

San Juan Public Lands Center
(USFS/BLM)
15 Burnett Ct.
Durango, CO 81301
(970) 247-4874
fax (970) 385-1375
www.co.blm.gov/sjra/index.html

Anasazi Heritage Center/Canyons of
the Ancients National Monument
27501 Hwy. 184
Dolores, CO 81323
(970) 882-4811
fax (970) 882-7035
www.co.blm.gov/ahc/index.htm

Royal Gorge Field Office—Front
Range Center (BLM/USFS)
3170 E. Main St.
Cañon City, CO 81212
(719) 269-8500
fax (719) 269-8599
http://www.blm.gov/co/st/en/fo/
rgfo.html

La Jara Field Office (BLM/USFS)
15571 County Rd. T5
La Jara, CO 81140
(719) 274-8971
fax (719) 274-6301
www.co.blm.gov/lajara/lajarahome.htm

Saguache Field Office (BLM/USFS)
46525 Hwy 114
PO Box 67
Saguache, CO 81149
(719) 655-2547
fax (719) 655-2502

www.co.blm.gov/saguache/
saghome.htm

Western Slope Center
2815 H Rd.
Grand Junction, CO 81506
(970) 244-3000
fax (970) 244-3083
www.co.blm.gov/wsc/index.html

Arkansas Headwaters Recreation
Area (State Parks/BLM)
307 W. Sackett Ave.
PO Box 126
Salida, CO 81201
(719) 539-7289
fax (719) 539-3771
parks.state.co.us

Columbine Field Office
(BLM/USFS)
110 W. 11th St.
Durango, CO 81301
(970) 385-1368
fax (970) 385-1375

Pagosa Field Office (BLM/USFS)
PO Box 310
Pagosa Springs, CO 81147
(970) 264-2268
fax (970) 264-1538

Del Norte Field Office (BLM/USFS)
13308 W. Hwy. 160
Del Norte, CO 81132
(719) 657-3321
fax (719) 657-6035

Mancos/Dolores Field Office
    (BLM/USFS)
100 N. Sixth St.
PO Box 210
Dolores, CO 81323
(970) 882-7296
fax (970) 882-6841

Front Range Center (BLM/USFS)
1803 W. Hwy. 160
Monte Vista, CO 81144
(719) 852-5941
fax (719) 852-6250

Colorado Canyons National
    Conservation Area
2815 H Rd.
Grand Junction, CO 81506
(970) 244-3000
fax (970) 244-3083
www.co.blm.gov/colocanyons/
index.htm

Gunnison Gorge National
    Conservation Area
2505 S. Townsend St.
Montrose, CO 81401
(970) 240-5300
fax (970) 240-5367
www.co.blm.gov/ggnca/index.htm

APPENDIX D: COUNTY OFFICE CONTACT INFORMATION

Adams
County Administration Building
(303) 659-2120

Alamosa
County Courthouse
(719) 589-3841

Arapahoe
County Administration Building
(303) 795-4630

Archuleta
County Courthouse
(970) 264-2536

Baca
County Courthouse
(719) 523-6532

Bent
County Courthouse
(719) 456-1600

Boulder
County Courthouse
(303) 441-3500

Broomfield
City and County Offices
(303) 469-3301

Chaffee
County Courthouse
(719) 539-2218

Cheyenne
County Courthouse
(719) 767-5872

Clear Creek
County Courthouse
(303) 569-3251

Conejos
County Courthouse
(719) 376-5772

Costilla
County Courthouse
(719) 672-3372

Crowley
County Courthouse
(719) 267-3248

Custer
County Courthouse
(719) 783-2552

Delta
County Courthouse
(970) 874-2101

Denver
City and County Building
(720) 913-4900

Dolores
County Courthouse
(970) 677-2383

Douglas
County Administration Building
(303) 660-7400

Eagle
County Administration Building
(970) 328-8600

El Paso
County Office Building
(719) 520-6400

Elbert
County Courthouse
(303) 621-2341

Fremont
County Courthouse
(719) 276-7330

Garfield
County Courthouse
(970) 945-5004

Gilpin
County Courthouse
(303) 582-5214

Grand
County Courthouse
(970) 725-3347

Gunnison
County Courthouse
(970) 641-0248

Hinsdale
County Courthouse
(970) 944-2225

Huerfano
County Courthouse
(719) 738-2370

Jackson
County Courthouse
(970) 723-4334

Jefferson
County Government Center
(303) 271-8525

Kiowa
County Courthouse
(719) 438-5810

Kit Carson
County Courthouse
(719) 346-8133

La Plata
County Courthouse
(970) 382-6219

Lake
County Courthouse
(719) 486-0993

Larimer
County Courthouse
(970) 498-7010

Las Animas
County Courthouse
(719) 845-1630

Lincoln
County Courthouse
(719) 743-2842

Logan
County Courthouse
(970) 522-0888

Mesa
County Courthouse
(970) 244-1602

Mineral
County Courthouse
(719) 658-2331

Moffat
County Courthouse
(970) 824-5517

Montezuma
County Courthouse
(970) 565-8317

Montrose
County Courthouse
(970) 249-7755

Morgan
County Courthouse
(970) 542-3414

Otero
County Courthouse
(719) 383-3000

Ouray
County Courthouse
(970) 325-4961

Park
County Courthouse
(719) 836-2771

Phillips
County Courthouse
(970) 854-2454

Pitkin
County Courthouse
(970) 920-5200

Prowers
County Courthouse
(719) 336-8025

Pueblo
County Courthouse
(719) 583-6000

Rio Blanco
County Courthouse
(970) 878-5001

Rio Grande
County Courthouse
(719) 657-2744

Routt
County Courthouse
(970) 879-0108

Saguache
County Courthouse
(719) 655-2231

San Juan
County Courthouse
(970) 387-5766

San Miguel
County Courthouse
(970) 728-3844

Sedgwick
County Courthouse
(970) 474-2485

Summit
County Courthouse
(970) 453-2561

Teller
County Courthouse
(719) 689-2988

Washington
County Courthouse
(970) 345-2701

Weld
Centennial Center
(970) 351-4000

Yuma
County Courthouse
(970) 332-5796

APPENDIX E: NATIONAL FOREST CONTACT INFORMATION

Arapaho and Roosevelt National
Forests and Pawnee National
Grassland
Boulder Ranger District
(303) 541-2500

Canyon Lakes Ranger District
(970) 498-2770

Clear Creek Ranger District
(303) 567-3000

Sulphur Ranger District
(970) 887-4100

Pawnee National Grassland
(970) 353-5004

Comanche National Grassland
La Junta
(719) 384-2181

Springfield
(719) 523-6591

Pike and San Isabel National Forests
Leadville Ranger District
(719) 486-0749

Pikes Peak Ranger District
(719) 636-1602

Salida Ranger District
(719) 539-3591

San Carlos Ranger District
(719) 269-8500

South Park Ranger District
(719) 836-2031

South Platte Ranger District
(303) 275-5610

Rio Grande National Forest
Office of the Supervisor
(719) 852-5941

Conejos Peak Ranger District
(719) 274-8971

Divide Ranger District (Creede)
(719) 658-2556

Divide Ranger District (Del Norte)
(719) 657-3321

Saguache Ranger District
(719) 655-2547

Grand Mesa, Uncompahgre, and
Gunnison National Forests
Office of the Supervisor
(970) 874-6600

Grand Mesa National Forest
Collbran Ranger District
(970) 487-3534

Grand Junction Ranger District
(970) 242-8411

Uncompahgre National Forest
Norwood Ranger District
(970) 327-4261

Ouray Ranger District
(970) 240-5300

Gunnison National Forest
Paonia Ranger District
(970) 527-4131

Taylor River/Cebolla Ranger
   District
(970) 641-0471

Routt National Forest
Hahns Peak/Bears Ears Ranger
   District
(970) 879-1870

Parks Ranger District
(970) 723-8204 (Walden)
(970) 724-3437 (Kremmling)

Yampa Ranger District
(970) 638-4516

San Juan National Forest
Columbine East Ranger District
   (Bayfield)
(970) 884-2512

Columbine West Ranger District
   (Durango)
(970) 884-2512

Dolores Ranger District
(970) 882-7296

Pagosa Ranger District
(970) 264-2268

White River National Forest
Office of the Supervisor
(970) 945-2521

Aspen Ranger District
(970) 925-3445

Blanco Ranger District
(970) 878-4039

Dillon Ranger District
(970) 468-5400

Eagle Ranger District
(970) 328-6388

Holy Cross Ranger District
(970) 827-5715

Rifle Ranger District
(970) 625-2371

Sopris Ranger District
(970) 963-2266

INDEX

Page numbers in italics refer to figures.

ABOUT THE AUTHORS

William A. Kappele has been rockhounding across the West for more than forty years. His other books include *Rockhounding Nevada* and *Rockhounding Utah*.

Gary Warren and his wife, Sally Warren, have been rockhounders for many years. They live in Brigham City, Utah, and have 4 children, 15 grandchildren, and 7 great-grandchildren. They have been members of the Cache Rock and Gem Club in Logan, Utah, for 17 years, and Gary has been the president of this club for 14 of those years. Gary enjoys sharing his love of rockhounding with children through school lectures and after-school group demonstrations and activities. He now teaches a rockhounding class at Utah State University. Each year, the Cache Rock and Gem Club hosts a rock show in May with a regular attendance of over 3,000 people. The club has also incorporated a junior rockhounding program to help teach kids about rocks and encourage them to pursue this hobby. Gary and Sally are semiretired and enjoy taking time to pursue their passions of travel and rockhounding. This hobby came in handy when Gary was asked to revise the *Rockhounding Utah* guidebook. Since that was completed and updated, he has also revised this guide (*Rockhounding Colorado*) and the *Rockhounding Nevada* guidebook.